WITH

3 PARA

TO THE FALKLANDS

**For my children
Ben, Emily and Charlotte**

WITH
3 PARA
TO THE FALKLANDS

GRAHAM COLBECK

Greenhill Books, London
Stackpole Books, Pennsylvania

With 3 Para to the Falklands first published 2002 by
Greenhill Books, Lionel Leventhal Limited, Park House,
1 Russell Gardens, London NW11 9NN
www.greenhillbooks.com
and
Stackpole Books, 5067 Ritter Road, Mechanicsburg, PA 17055, USA

British Library Cataloguing in Publication Data
Colbeck, Graham
With 3 Para to the Falklands
1. Colbeck, Graham 2. Great Britain. Army. Parachute Regiment. Battalion, 3rd
3. Falkland Islands War, 1982–
Personal narratives, British
I. Title
997.1'1024'092

ISBN 1-85367-493-1

Library of Congress Cataloging-in-Publication Data available

Typeset by DP Photosetting, Aylesbury, Bucks
Printed and bound in Great Britain
by CPD (Wales), Ebbw Vale

Contents

List of Maps

List of Illustrations

All photographs are the author's copyright except no. 38 (photographer unknown).

Glossary and Abbreviations

AFV	Armoured Fighting Vehicle.
AOA	Amphibious Operations Area.
ATGW	Anti-tank Guided Weapon.
Atts	Attachments.
Bandwagon	Also known as 'BV'. A tracked, articulated over-snow vehicle built in Sweden and used by the British Army and Marines.
Bellerophon	Mythical Corinthian hero. Rode Pegasus in his victory over the fire-breathing Chimaera.
Bergen	A large army rucksack.
Bivvy	A small shelter constructed from an issued waterproof 'poncho' or similar.
Blowpipe	British surface-to-air missile, shoulder-launched.
Blue-on-Blue	A mistaken engagement between men of the same side. 'Blue forces' was the term given to 'friendly' forces on exercises, the enemy were 'Red' (now changed to a more politically correct 'Orange').
C130	US-built 'Hercules' heavy-lift transport aircraft used by British and Argentine air forces.
Camp	Falkland Islands term for all areas outside Stanley.
Carl Gustav	An 84mm recoilless anti-tank weapon, firing a projectile with a HEAT warhead.
Casevac	Casualty evacuation.
Cdo	Commando.
Chinook	Giant twin-rotor support helicopter. Designed and built in the USA and used by both British and Argentine forces.
Civvies	Civilians, or civilian clothes.
CO	Commanding Officer (of a Battalion) – usually a Lieutenant-Colonel.

9

Company	Sub-unit of a Battalion. Each of the 3 Rifle Companies of 3 Para consisted of 3 Platoons and a Headquarters commanded by a Major.
Contact	An encounter with the enemy.
Cross-deck	To move personnel or stores from one ship to another.
CQMS	Company Quarter Master Sergeant.
CVR(T)	Combat Vehicle Reconnaissance (Tracked). British light armoured vehicle, such as Scorpion, with a 76mm gun, Scimitar, with a 30mm cannon, and the Samson recovery vehicle.
Dets	Detachments.
DMS	Direct Moulded Sole. Boots worn by Paras and infantry units in the Falklands – generally considered to have been unsuitable for the climate and the terrain.
DZ	Drop Zone – ground designated for parachutists or parachute-borne vehicles/ammunition/stores.
Exocet	French designed and built anti-ship missile. Launched from land, sea or air.
FGA	Fighter Ground Attack.
Gp	Group.
GPMG	General Purpose Machine-Gun. A belt-fed 7.62mm weapon, normally used by the firer in the lying position, supported on its integral bipod, but could be fired from other positions, including from the hip when standing. The same weapon could be converted to the 'Sustained Fire' role – see SF.
GR	'Grid' map reference.
GSM	General Service Medal.
Harrier	British combat aircraft used by the RAF and Fleet Air Arm. The Navy version was known as Sea Harrier. Responsible for 22 'kills' of Argentine aircraft. Six Harriers were lost – two in accidents, four due to ground fire.
HE	High Explosive.
HEAT	High Explosive Anti-tank. A warhead with a shaped charge designed to penetrate armour.
Heraclitus	Greek philosopher c. 500 BC. Believed things in the

	world were divided into opposites, and that change, or 'strife', was necessary for their continued unification.
Hercules	See C130.
HESH	High Explosive Squash Head. A warhead designed to fracture armour.
Hexamine	Small solid-fuel block used to heat food/water.
H-hour	The time at which attacking troops cross their Start Line or disembark from their landing craft.
ID	Identity.
IWS	Individual Weapon Sight. British image-intensifier night sight used on SLR and GPMG – inferior to similar sights used by the Argentines.
JR	Junior Ranks.
LCU	Landing Craft Utility. Capable of carrying 200 men or 22 tons of vehicles/stores. Four LCUs were carried inside each LPD.
LCVP	Landing Craft Vehicle and Personnel. Capable of carrying 30 men or a small vehicle. Four LCVPs were carried on each LPD.
Loadie	Loadmaster.
LPD	Landing Platform Dock. Assault ship – there were two in the Task Force, *Fearless* and *Intrepid*. Each carried eight landing craft.
LSL	Landing Ship Logistic. A Royal Fleet Auxiliary roll-on, roll-off support ship.
Lt Col	Lieutenant-Colonel.
Lt Gen	Lieutenant-General.
MAPCO	System for encoding map references.
MFC	Mortar Fire Controller; usually a Corporal.
Milan	Missile Infantry Light ANti-tank. A portable anti-tank guided weapon system with a range of 1,950 metres, used in the Falklands against enemy bunkers and other ground targets.
Mirage	A French-built fighter bomber jet aircraft used by the Argentine Air Force – 19 lost in war.
MMG	Medium Machine-Gun (see also SF).
MV	Motor Vessel.
NAAFI	Naval, Army and Air Force Institute.

NBC	Nuclear, Biological, Chemical.
NCO	Non-Commissioned Officer.
NGFO	Naval Gunfire Observer. An artillery officer whose role was to direct the gunfire of ships and artillery.
NOD	Night Observation Device – specifically a large British image-intensifier, used hand-held or on a small tripod.
OC	Officer Commanding (of a Company) – usually a Major.
O Group	Orders Group. A meeting of sub-unit commanders in which formal orders are given to them by their commander.
OP	Observation Post. A hidden position occupied by a small patrol of men, from which to observe an area and report back information by radio.
Op	Operation – a planned military task – in the British Army given a one-word codename.
Orbat	Order of Battle. The breakdown of sub-units within a fighting force.
Padre	Army chaplain. One served with each Battalion.
Password	Actually two words, a codeword used as a verbal challenge to an unidentified individual, usually at night, and another word with which the challenged individual would be expected to reply.
P Company	Pre-Parachute Company. Airborne Forces selection course.
Pegasus	Winged horse of Greek mythology, born of the blood which flowed from the head of the Gorgon Medusa when it was cut off by Perseus.
Platoon	Infantry grouping of 3 Sections plus a Headquarters commanded by a Lieutenant or Second-Lieutenant with a strength of around 30 men. Platoons were numbered consecutively, i.e. A Company had 1, 2 and 3; B Company 4, 5 and 6; C Company 7, 8 and 9. Support Company Platoons had different groupings – the Anti-tank Platoon of 3 Para was 50 strong.
POW	Prisoner of War.
PT	Physical Training.

Pucara	Argentinian designed and built twin turbo-prop close support/reconnaissance aircraft. 14 lost and 14 captured in Falklands Campaign.
QM	Quartermaster. Officer responsible for logistics within a Battalion. Usually a Captain.
Range Card	A plan drawn by the occupants of each infantry trench showing the arc of fire and distances to points within it.
RAP	Regimental Aid Post. A casualty treatment post at Battalion level.
Rapier	British land-based surface-to-air missile.
RAS	Replenishment At Sea.
Recce	Reconnaissance.
REME	Royal Electrical and Mechanical Engineers.
REMF	Rear Echelon Mother-Fucker. Term applied by combat soldiers to those soldiers without a front line combat role.
RFA	Royal Fleet Auxiliary.
RHA	Royal Horse Artillery.
RSM	Regimental Sergeant Major. The senior non-commissioned rank.
RV	Rendezvous.
Sangar	A defensive emplacement built above ground level, usually of rocks.
SAS	Special Air Service.
SBS	Special Boat Squadron.
Sea King	Support helicopter – designed in the USA and British built. Workhorse of the Task Force.
Section	Smallest sub-grouping of infantry, usually eight men, but often more in support weapons teams. Each of the nine Rifle Platoons numbered its Sections 1, 2 and 3. In Support Company, the Milan Section of 3 Para was 19 men strong.
Senior Ranks	Non-commissioned ranks of Sergeant and above.
SF	Sustained Fire. A GPMG in the SF role would be mounted on a heavy tripod allowing more accurate, heavier firing over extended periods and ranges.
Skyhawk	Argentine jet-propelled attack aircraft – 20 lost in war.

13

SLIDEX   A radio code system.

SLR   Self-Loading Rifle. British 7.62mm semi-automatic rifle fed by a 20-round magazine. The Argentines used a similar weapon with the advantage of a fully automatic capability.

SMG   Sub-Machine Gun. The British SMG was the Sterling 9mm with a 30-round magazine.

SP   Support (as in SP Company).

SSAFA   Soldiers', Sailors' and Airmen's Families Association.

Stag   A period of sentry duty, usually two hours. To be 'on stag' was to be a sentry.

Start Line A line on the ground designated as the point that attacking troops will cross at H-Hour. Usually a natural feature such as a stream or a track.

Stinger   US designed and built shoulder-launched surface-to air missile. Used by an SAS soldier to shoot down a Pucara.

Stuft   Ship taken up from trade – merchant ship on charter.

Tab   Para slang for march/walk. Originally 'Tactical Advance to Battle'.

Tank deck   Lower deck on LPD.

Tom/Toms   Slang for a Parachute Regiment private soldier, or soldiers in general below the rank of Sergeant.

Turner Prize Annual award for British contemporary art.

VC10   British jet airliner used by the RAF.

VOCAB   A radio code system.

Webbing   Individual equipment worn in battle consisting of a belt with pouches for ammunition, water bottles and other items supported by shoulder straps, to which a pick or a shovel was attached.

Wessex   British support helicopter. Long-serving and tried and trusted.

Wombat   A British 120mm recoilless anti-tank weapon. Taken to the Falklands on *Canberra* but never left the ship.

Z (Zulu)   Referring to Greenwich Mean Time, the time used by all British Forces during the Campaign, even though local time in the Falklands was four hours behind GMT. Timings on the Falklands in this book are referred to in local time unless suffixed by 'Z'.

Foreword

Lieutenant-General Sir Hew Pike, KCB, DSO, MBE

Graham Colbeck was one of the outstanding figures in 3 Para during the Falklands Campaign of 1982. As a Sergeant in the Milan Anti-tank Platoon, he applied his experience and exceptional technical expertise with a resourcefulness and determination that marked him out as a leader to whom others increasingly turned, as the conditions of war became more difficult. Whether working out the best way of man-packing firing posts, requisitioning tractors and sledges for the supply of missiles needed by the Battalion, or constructing a bigger bunker than anyone else when we were in defence, his talents were always to the fore. He was also one of the few people who managed to keep up a diary, which is the basis of this book.

For those involved, the Falklands War was probably the most intense and vivid experience of a lifetime, the more so because it was unexpected. At the same time, it provided a unique chance to prove professional skills, and to practise 'for real' those tasks which had been the substance of so many exercises. Furthermore, the situation and the terrain seemed to be almost 'tailor made' for airborne and commando forces. The will to win was therefore formidable, and nowhere more so than in 3 Para, who marched – or 'tabbed' as we call it – from Port San Carlos to Port Stanley and fought one of the crucial battles of the Campaign, to capture Mount Longdon.

Graham Colbeck's book gives an insight into the realities of war and infantry soldiering, and should be read by any soldier who wants to understand how to make training not a mere substitute for war, but a demanding and constructive preparation for it.

Hew Pike
March 2002

Soldiers are citizens of death's grey land,
Drawing no dividend from time's to-morrows.
In the great hour of destiny they stand,
Each with his feuds, and jealousies, and sorrows.

Siegfried Sassoon, 'Dreamers'

Prologue

Truth after all is always so much more than fact.
                    Laurens Van Der Post, *The Night of the New Moon*

On 22 October 1992, over ten years after the battle of Mount Longdon, two detectives from the International and Organised Crime Squad of the Metropolitan Police arrived at my home in North Yorkshire. They were preparing a report for the Director of Public Prosecutions concerning allegations of war crimes by the Third Battalion of the Parachute Regiment (3 Para) during the Falklands Campaign in 1982. I had served as a Sergeant in 3 Para during the Campaign and I was to be questioned as a possible witness to alleged atrocities against Argentinian prisoners after the Mount Longdon battle. Having witnessed nothing but humane treatment of prisoners I was little help to the detectives, who left with my large collection of Falklands photographs as an 'exhibit'.

During my questioning the detectives unrolled two large photographs and spread them on my lounge floor. They were pictures of Mount Longdon taken from the air, and my first thought on seeing them was how useful they would have been if they had been available to us before the battle. The air photographs showed the whole length of the hill in great detail – a hill that we had fought to capture at great cost on the night of 11 June 1982. Although ten years had passed since the battle, looking at the photographs made it seem as if it had happened only the week before.

I was asked to point out on the air photographs and mark the positions where each of my own photographs had been taken from, and indicate the direction I had been facing for each shot. I was also asked to indicate the location of a feature on Mount Longdon that, since the battle, had been labelled 'the bowl' and had gained notoriety as the place where the hardest fighting took place. Finding the bowl on the photograph proved to be an unexpectedly difficult task, and I first confused the area with a similar feature further to the east, correcting my mistake later when I identified the 'sangar', or defensive emplacement, in which I had sheltered at the edge of the bowl with two other 3 Para men after the battle.

Along with my photographs, the detectives also took a copy of the privately published account of my Falklands experiences, from which this revised and expanded story has been born. At the time of writing over nineteen years have passed since the events I describe, but although some of my memories of those days seem as vivid as ever, it appears as if the great adventure we embarked upon is only a story in a *Boy's Own Annual*, belonging to an altogether different era; a time of Queen Victoria and Empire and maps shaded pink; an unseemly squabble over distant, relatively insignificant islands fought for the pride of the Land of Hope and Glory.

The Duke of Wellington likened the history of a battle to the history of a ball; it is almost impossible to describe accurately what happened when, or to say exactly where a certain incident took place, or who was involved at each stage. Each man involved remembers a different version of the same event, and no doubt believes sincerely that his memory of it is the true picture.

Wars are inevitable. Man will always tend to resort to violence as a way of solving disputes until the day when he might somehow be genetically modified to remove the violent animal in him – and if the day ever comes when permanent worldwide peace is assured and taken for granted, then war must be replaced by some other threat or there would be nothing to put a necessary tension into life. These sayings of the philosopher Heraclitus make perfect sense to me: 'Two men saw a log. One pushes while the other pulls, but in doing so they are doing the same thing. While making more they are making less. Such is the nature of man', and, 'If it were not for injustice men would not know justice.' There must be balance in the world. Joy and Sorrow. Love and Hate. Peace and War.

The word 'war' comes from the Anglo-Saxon 'wyrre', meaning 'confusion'. Officially, our battles and manoeuvrings to recapture the Falkland Islands could not be called a war, since war was not declared, but the 'Falklands Campaign', as it was known, was for those at the sharp end as confusing as a war can get. The battle for Mount Longdon, fought in darkness over broken, rocky terrain, could be described in the same terms as the mist-shrouded Crimean

War Battle of Inkermann as a 'Soldier's Battle' – effective command and control being impossible for much of the time. Accounts of the battle differ. I, of course, believe my version of events to be true, but no doubt there will be those who remember things differently; certainly, from some of the accounts I have read it would appear to be so. Even the 'official' history of the battle does not, to my recollection, give an entirely accurate account of the events; but perhaps that is not important – perhaps what actually happened matters less than what those who took part *believe to have happened*. The battle is the sum of the experiences of all who fought in it, including those who died in it.

I remember a rather vague warning that filtered down to me from a higher level of command during our approach to the Falkland Islands, prohibiting the carrying of personal cameras once ashore. The good reason given for this order was that exposed film could provide the enemy with useful information if they captured it. Since the warning was more of a rumour than an actual order I chose to ignore it – if members of the press were to be allowed to film and photograph the Task Force it did not make much sense to stop soldiers doing so. Interestingly, copies of the photographs I took during the Campaign were much in demand from some of the Battalion's senior officers after our return to England.

I heard no warnings about keeping diaries, which could have been banned with more justification, and any doubts I may have had about taking my diary ashore were dispelled when I saw that both my Company Commander and Sergeant-Major had both done the same. I felt obliged to keep a record of what promised to be a unique experience in my life and the result has formed the basis of what follows – not a comprehensive account of 3 Para's role in Operation Corporate (as the Campaign was named) but a portrait of life with the Battalion as I experienced it. The picture is an honest one, and I have included the warts – for no military unit is ever perfect. I should add that the opinions expressed here are entirely my own, and do not necessarily represent the views of the Parachute Regiment.

Seen against the three-hundred-year history of the British Army at war, the Battle of Mount Longdon would probably rate as little more than a skirmish; but even so, to those involved in the thickest of the fighting it was a frighteningly intense and bloody affair. As soldiers we went to war because warfare was our profession, because we were paid to fight. We went to war to save British subjects from an imposed fascist dictatorship. We went to war for the sake of national honour; but when it came to the actual fighting all these things were far from our minds and counted for nothing – we fought for ourselves, but more than that – we fought, as soldiers always have done, for each other.

1. AIRBORNE

I am a soldier,
A name that in my thoughts becomes me best.

William Shakespeare, *Henry V*

————— ·◆· —————

A chill wind blew across the rocky hillside where we had stopped to rest. Now that we were cloaked in darkness and free from the blistering heat of the day, we were able to move faster and use less of our precious water.

I unscrewed the cap of one of my metal water bottles and took a mouthful of refreshingly cool water.

I was still wearing my Airborne issue, camouflaged pattern 'Dennison Smock' next to my skin; this had made me far too warm during the day, but now I considered taking my shirt from my pack to wear as well. Being a new boy, or 'crow', I waited to see what the others would do. They remained dressed as I was – they knew that once we started tabbing again we would soon be warm enough.

As I observed my 'arc of fire' (each man faced outwards for 'all-round defence'), I looked down on a small village in the valley below. A few lights were visible, but it was very late and most of the inhabitants would have been asleep. I thought about the life I had chosen for myself – so different from the lives of ordinary people, or 'civvies'. I was seventeen. I carried a rifle, and with another four hundred or so armed men, moved unnoticed through the hills and valleys of a remote area of Cyprus, while 'normal' people were in bed.

I was taking part in my first field exercise with my Battalion, 3 Para. It was the summer of 1970 and I had recently 'passed out' of the Parachute Regiment Depot in Aldershot before joining 3 Para in Malta. In those days the tiny island of Malta was garrisoned by two British infantry battalions, and 3 Para was over halfway through a two-year posting to the island. Malta was too small an island for large-scale military training and so we had flown to Cyprus, arrived by parachute and were now approaching the end of a long 'tab', our ultimate goal being the destruction of an 'enemy' comprising scattered groups of wooden targets. There was no 'live' enemy force on this particular exercise, and so we carried live ammunition to be used in the planned attack.

The following day B Company advanced along a valley as part of a Battalion 'Advance to Contact'. High on the slopes on either side of us I could see small groups of men; these were the patrols of D (Patrol) Company picketing the high ground to cover our advance.

This was my first experience of a military manoeuvre on this scale, and it made a deep impression on me. I was fascinated by the fact that although I was an individual human being, capable of independent thought and action, I was in fact subordinate to something much greater and more important than myself – the Battalion, and I was controlled by its command system. I was simply one of several hundred parts of this great bloodthirsty beast which lived and moved and fought as one entity, with a central nervous system all of its own; a creature which was able to survive the loss of one or many of its parts and carry on until its destructive mission was complete.

I knew then that I made the right choice when I had enlisted in the Parachute Regiment. This was what I was intended to be; this was my destiny – to be a necessary yet expendable part of this magnificent warlike animal that was certain of its superiority in a world of similar but inferior animals. Lord of the jungle. Challenge me if you dare – I will brush you aside and turn to face the next threat.

I had enlisted in the Army immediately after leaving school and having chosen to become a paratrooper I was sent to the Para Depot at Aldershot where I joined a recruit platoon to begin my basic training.

Why did I choose the Parachute Regiment? If asked at the time I would have probably said, 'Because it's the best regiment in the Army', or, 'Because I wanted a challenge', or something equally misleading. The fact is that young men of a certain character are naturally drawn to the Paras; men who share a restless and reckless spirit; who are not yet ready, and perhaps never will be, to 'settle down' in a steady job with a safe and predictable routine. Men who are still boys with a taste for adventure – searching for something as yet unknown and elusive. Perhaps looking for an answer to the question, 'What kind of man am I?' Looking for an identity – or perhaps looking to lose one or cloak it in Army camouflage. Looking, in many cases, for a home and a family. Lost boys; diverse characters but sharing, to a greater or lesser extent, a need to prove something to themselves and perhaps to others; to put themselves to the test and to experience a way of life outside the accepted norm.

The military life was not 'in my blood' – at least there appears to have been little history of Army service in my family. My male ancestors had, for almost two hundred years, been Yorkshire coal-miners or mill-workers. My paternal grandfather served, reluctantly I believe, in the Great War for two years as a Royal Field Artillery gunner on the Western Front, and he still carried fragments of shrapnel around in his leg. He told me nothing about that time apart from the fact that he went 'AWOL' from training and was caught by Military Police in Ripon. If I inherited anything of use to me in my chosen career as a paratrooper it was a capacity for hard physical work.

My recruit platoon at Aldershot was, at the start of training after many hopefuls had been weeded out, 44 strong. Aged from 17 to around 25, of various shapes and sizes and from all parts of the United Kingdom, we assembled under a staff consisting of an officer, a sergeant and three corporals, who would all in their various ways attempt to reduce our number by all the means at their disposal – to weed out those who did not deserve to wear the famous red beret and parachute 'wings'.

Sure enough, it was not long before men began to drop out of the training, either by choice or by failing to meet the standards in one way or another. The training, which took place in and around Aldershot and at the Para 'Battle School' in South Wales, consisted of a mixture of physical training, weapons and tactical training, map reading, radio communications, drill and 'bullshit', all combined with what could be termed, 'indoctrination'.

We learned the Second World War battle honours of our young (for the British Army) Regiment, and we were shown films of past campaigns. I still remember a phrase used by the narrator of one of the films that described an action in the Radfan Mountains when 3

Para had come under fire from a rebel position: 'being paratroopers they immediately attacked'. That phrase has always seemed to me to embody the ethos of the Parachute Regiment. We were also told that in order to become paratroopers we must possess a quality known as, 'Airborne Initiative', and be able to act without orders if necessary if we found ourselves alone when dropped behind enemy lines.

After about eight weeks of initial training those of us who remained in Recruit Platoon number 349 were ready to face 'Pre-Parachute Company', or 'P Company' as it was known; several days of gruelling physical tests. This was the stage of training when we infantry soldiers were pitted against men from other arms – gunners, medics, engineers, and so on, who aspired to join Airborne Forces and serve in 16 Para Brigade. A series of individual and team events such as the Log Race, the Steeplechase and 'Milling' (high-speed boxing with non-stop punching) took place.

At the end of each event the winning team would be presented with the P Company pennant to carry back to barracks, and after one of the events the honour fell to me. I ran at the head of the Platoon holding the staff with its maroon and blue pennant topped by the winged horse, Pegasus – carrying Bellerophon with his spear held aloft, the symbol of British Airborne Forces. I had never felt so proud.

Those of us who passed P Company were sent to RAF Abingdon in Oxfordshire to qualify as parachutists. We were trained by RAF PJIs – Parachute Jump Instructors – who wore badges with the motto, 'Knowledge Dispels Fear' – well, maybe.

After several days of rolling around on mats, jumping from plywood aircraft mock-ups and falling from various contraptions we were ready for our first 'jump' from a balloon. The helium-filled balloon, looking just like a Second World War barrage balloon (which it probably was) rose slowly to the height of 800 feet at the end of steel cable winched out from the back of a lorry on the flat green turf of Weston-on-the-Green DZ. Beneath the balloon hung a 'cage' – a square platform with small wooden walls around it, and an open 'door' in one side. Inside the cage as it lifted and swayed were five intrepid would-be paratroopers including myself – all fear, of course, by now dispelled by the knowledge instilled in us by our PJI, who nonchalantly leaned out of the door.

At 800 feet above the earth, when the winch motor had stopped and an eerie silence tended to concentrate the mind, the first man was called to the door after checking that his static line was firmly attached to the metal bar above. I would have preferred to go first, but waited in my corner and watched the parachute of the man in the door, finding that better than looking at the roofs of the tiny cars on the roads below. 'GO!' – and out from the womb he went, the cage swaying even more now as the PJI hauled in the limp umbilical cord, an empty parachute bag on the end of it. My turn. Trying to remember the simple drills, I edged forward to the door and positioned the toecap of my forward boot over the edge of the platform. He must have said, 'GO!' – because I found myself trying, but failing, to open my eyes as the contents of my abdomen tried to force their way through my diaphragm and my parachute rigging lines rattled the back of my steel helmet. After what seemed like about ten minutes of speeding earthwards I became aware that I could breathe again and I was gently floating beneath a great nylon umbrella. Someone on the ground was shouting instructions at me through a megaphone. I carried out the required drills and prepared to hit the earth, thinking the words I used on that and all subsequent jumps to ready myself for impact, 'Head down, shoulders round, knees bent and watch the ground' – not something my instructors had taught me but something I had read in a book somewhere (knowledge dispels fear). The grass rushed up at me and I collapsed in an ungainly sort of mimicry of a textbook parachute roll. Easy, really.

After a second jump, again from a balloon but with more apprehension beforehand, knowing what to expect (the same is probably true of fighting battles), we jumped from an Argosy aircraft and then from the ubiquitous C130 Hercules, by day and then by night, qualifying for our parachute wings before returning to Aldershot to complete our training.

On the whole, apart from some of the physical tests and part of the winter field exercises at the Parachute Regiment Battle School in Wales, I did not find my time at the depot very difficult. I was helped by the fact that I had been an Army Cadet and I had already learned the rudiments of infantry soldiering in the King's Own Yorkshire Light Infantry under tuition of instructors with Second World War experience. The KOYLI cap badge and proud motto, 'Cede Nullis' –

'Yield to None' – have long since disappeared from the Army through disbandment and amalgamations.

There were 11 recruits remaining in our recruit platoon, and I found that I had been awarded the trophy for 'Champion Recruit' as well as for 'Champion Rifle Shot'. Having been mildly surprised to win two trophies I was then annoyed with myself for not doing better in the machine-gun competition – I was only one shot behind the winner of that trophy.

Proudly wearing our red berets and parachute wings we were sent to join 3 Para in Malta, returning to a chilly Aldershot six months later. The winter of 1970/71 is stuck in my memory as the time I endured the hardest field training I have ever experienced. A Battalion drop on to Sennybridge Army training area in South Wales was planned, followed by a tactical exercise lasting several days. Due to appalling weather the drop was cancelled, so we 'jumped' from coaches and trucks spread out along a road running through the DZ. There followed a succession of night 'tabs', or marches, interspersed with digging waterlogged holes and inhabiting them, all of it undertaken (at least in my case as a lowly 'Tom'), with little idea why. There was no 'enemy' and no apparent point to the exercise, which became one of pure endurance. We were equipped and acclimatised for the Mediterranean area and after only two days the first exposure cases resulted, followed by men suffering from 'trench foot' – none of them allowed to be 'casevaced' to the training camp – they had to be treated in the field.

About the only information passed to us, rather boastfully, after several days in our muddy holes was that the SAS had been training in the same area and had gone back to barracks because of the severe weather. The worse the conditions became, and the more the men suffered, the more determined the Commanding Officer became to carry on with the 'training' – which ended, at last, after a long night march to camp in the continuing rain.

That night I awoke in my wooden hut in the training camp feeling as if the end of my mattress was on fire – my feet were red-hot and swollen, and I spent the rest of the night going to and from the showers to cool them down (the worst thing I could have done). At reveille next morning I found that my burning feet were so swollen that I had great difficulty putting on my boots. So this was trench foot.

I was determined not to 'go sick' and join the men in the over-crowded medical centre because I did not want to miss the rest of the training, which was in preparation for 3 Para's first tour of duty in Ulster.

——— •◆• ———

After being lectured on the background to the 'Troubles' and trying to understand why Protestants and Catholics hated each other so much, we got down to the practical side of 'peacekeeping', which seemed to require a lot of marching about in a box formation with a metal shield and a wooden stick. The tactics of the time were based on the Army's experience in Britain's troubled colonies around the world. Crowd control involved hitting a few rioters over the head and then, if that did not disperse them, an officer would shout a warning through his megaphone, the 'ringleader' would be identified and a soldier with a rifle would advance and shoot him dead. It seemed simple, except that we were given a list of rules based on 'minimum force' describing the circumstances in which we were allowed to open fire. Training for service in the Province would later become far more thorough and realistic, but in those early days each unit trained as it thought best – based on minimum experience and outdated drills.

We sailed to Belfast in early 1971, on one of the LSLs that would later be part of the Falklands Amphibious Task Group. B Company, to which I belonged, moved eventually to Ballymurphy and occupied a primary school and the adjacent Henry Taggart Hall, the whole complex having been recently surrounded by barbed wire and dotted with sandbagged sentry posts. In a rather bizarre arrangement, B Company slept in classrooms on the first floor of the school, and the children attended school as normal, using only the ground floor. My platoon lived in what had formerly been an art classroom, complete with all its art materials that we put to good use by painting elaborate and colourful pictures on the windowpanes to conceal our beds from the overlooking block of flats. The toilets and sinks were tiny, meant for young schoolchildren, and had the effect of making us feel gigantic. From this Lilliputian world we ventured out in Landrovers to be stoned by seven-year-olds, and stalked through the back gardens of the housing estates at night with blackened faces, earning ourselves the nickname, 'Flowerpot men'.

The infantry regiment that had been responsible for that part of Belfast before our arrival had declared the staunch Republican Ballymurphy Estate a 'no-go' area – in other words they had not gone into it, leaving its population to do as it pleased. We were having none of that, of course, and made a point of patrolling every part of the Estate at all times of the day or night. Our predecessors at the school had left behind pairs of homemade scrap-metal shin-guards on our beds; they had used the armour when they were called to a riot, where they would stand in line to be targets for bricks and Molotov cocktails. On discovering the armour we immediately threw it in the dustbin.

Long hours 'on stag' (sentry duty) in the sandbagged emplacements listening to gunshots and explosions that rocked the city were interspersed with patrolling, filling sandbags and erecting more barbed wire.

I missed my first chance to fire my rifle in anger during our stay at Ballymurphy: our base had been fired at once or twice at night from the Estate across the road, and our Company Commander decided to do something about it. His plan was to send my platoon out to work our way behind the gunman to seal his escape route. In order to leave our base unseen by the enemy, we travelled inside two armoured 'pigs' (armoured personnel carriers, or APCs) that set up a routine vehicle checkpoint near the Estate. We then slipped unnoticed from our Trojan Horse through a hedgerow and into a field bordering the houses. As we ran through gardens and jumped over barricades a shadowy figure carrying what looked like a rifle appeared on the footpath ahead of us. The Sergeant leading our group opened fire with his pistol at close range and the figure fell – I could have opened fire also but hesitated, trying to remember whether the 'Yellow Card' rules of engagement permitted me to shoot in the circumstances, by which time I had decided it was over – a shameful debut for a young warrior who dreamt of winning medals. On close inspection we found that our gunman had carried a shotgun and wore a bandolier of cartridges. Having tried to kill him we then saved his life by carrying him across to our base where he was given first aid and then taken to hospital. He was sixteen. I remember him crying for his mother.

The Army was constantly trying to develop better ways of dealing with the Northern Ireland situation, but in the very early 1970s we were really 'making it up as we went along'. Not long after our first tour of duty there it would have been considered the height of folly to go on patrol carrying only a pistol, as our Sergeant had.

I left Ulster, and 3 Para, to join an anti-tank missile platoon under command of Headquarters 16 Parachute Brigade. The 'Vigilant' wire-guided missile was a portable weapon that launched from a metal box. It required some dexterity on the part of the controller who had to guide the missile to its target by small movements of his thumb in a remote control unit. Having passed the aptitude test I joined Y Vigilant Platoon and spent the next six years there, sometimes training with one of the three parachute battalions and at other times independently, but always returning to Aldershot, where I would spend some of my spare time drinking, playing rugby, brawling and generally getting up to the kind of antics that a touring Heavy Metal rock band would have been proud of.

During my time at Aldershot I discovered that parachuting on a large scale was rather different to my experiences in training at Weston-on-the-Green. 16 Para Brigade and an RAF transport squadron formed what was known as UKJATFOR – UK Joint Airborne Task Force, which trained for a rapid reinforcement of troops by parachute into NATO countries that were about to be overrun by the Soviet hordes. We practised the deployment of the Airborne Task Force in England and then in Denmark and Germany. After preparing our Landrovers and trailers and then spending several hours 'rigging' them on a heavy drop platform so that they could also be deployed by parachute, we would pack our bergens and equipment and tie them up with straps fitted with hooks and a rope to attach to our parachute harnesses. Our weapons would be strapped to the side of our bergens. As well as personal weapons, ammunition, rations, water and equipment there were additional items to be carried such as mortars, 84mm rocket launchers, radios, batteries and the usual paraphernalia that the infantryman is burdened with. Wearing a steel helmet, lifejacket (in case of landing in the North Sea or similar), main and reserve parachutes, equipment and weapons we would be carrying upwards of 150 pounds in total.

——— •◆• ———

In my experience the airborne operation might go something like this: after many hours of preparation and checks, taking parachutes on and off, climbing on and off coaches or trucks I finally arrive at the rear of a waiting C130 Hercules with its rear ramp down, revealing four rows of aluminium and nylon seats. The camouflage painted, four-engined, turbo-prop aeroplane sits on the airfield at RAF Lyneham in Wiltshire along with 43 similar aircraft, some of them already loaded with parachute-fitted Landrovers, armoured cars or artillery howitzers. I take my place in one of the two lines of men and equipment. Each of the aircraft designated for personnel will carry 64 men in two 'sticks' – one stick will jump from each side of the plane. I am number 27 of the starboard stick, and my equipment and parachutes are checked again while the pilot starts the engines early so that we can all breathe and taste the acrid exhaust fumes and start to feel sick. I struggle up the ramp with my equipment into the belly of the aircraft where the 'loadie' and his crew somehow manage to squeeze 64 of us into a space that is surely meant for 30. There would be more room but the aircrew have brought their civvies in the hope that the aircraft will develop a fault after the drop, so that they can land at the airport of some foreign city and stay at a luxury hotel.

I am sat in one of the centre rows of seats touching knees with the outer row of men on the starboard side, and struggling with the man behind me in the port stick whose parachute is separated from mine by a thin nylon wall. The stink of aircraft fuel pervades the interior of the aircraft; an interior that gives the impression that it left the assembly line too early. Sweat escapes from my leather helmet-lining and runs over my camouflaged face as the engines whine and the rear ramp squeaks upwards before the plane lurches forward to join the others in a queue for the end of the runway. The roar of the engines increases and the aircraft rocks and demands that the brakes be released. We charge down the runway in our Pegasus and the acceleration bends us sideways towards the rear of the aircraft, which strains and then slowly points upwards before making banging, squeaking and assorted other noises which to the first-time traveller sound like the wheels have fallen off – in fact they are joining us inside.

We fly in formation – a line many miles long with aircraft in groups of six. We could be over Denmark in less than an hour but instead we have to prolong the agony by practising low-level flying over Devon, Wales and remote parts of Scotland. As the pilots enjoy themselves flying in valley bottoms 'to avoid radar' and try hard not to keep the wings horizontal for more than a few seconds at a time, their cargo is wondering why it ever considered becoming 'Airborne'. The man on my left is busy filling his sick bag; a man opposite tries to encourage him by simulating the act before pretending to drink it. Through a porthole I glimpse a white farmhouse above us on a hillside. My head aches. I want to get out.

After what seems like an age of torment the dispatchers start climbing about like monkeys and begin pulling the cables that will hold our static lines into position above us before shouting, 'Prepare for action!' I struggle to get my big foot through the loop in the leg strap of my equipment. There are more checks and then, 'Stand up! – Fit equipment!' – which is far easier said than done, but eventually I manage to attach a 100-pound bundle of equipment and rifle to my harness, and fit my reserve parachute above it. The seats are folded away. The full sick bags still kicking around on the floor are collected up by the crew. My spine feels compressed to a length of about one foot. The pilot manoeuvres the aircraft to stay in formation and I lurch against the side before correcting myself – then I am pushed backwards as the man in front falls against me. I clip my static line to the cable above and check the man in front. The dispatcher lifts my reserve and bangs the harness release box above my stomach with his fist – an act he only just survives without wearing my breakfast. I have over-tightened my helmet chinstrap and it refuses to be slackened – my skull protests. *I hate parachuting!*

'Tell-off for equipment check!' After the man behind hits my shoulder I hit the man in front and shout, 'Twenty-seven OK!' although I feel nothing like it. There is a mighty roar of in-rushing air as the jump doors are lifted at the end of the long rows of helmets in front of me, and the stale air inside becomes cool and fresh. The pilot throttles back to the jump speed which lowers the tail and makes our route to the door slightly downhill. 'Action Stations!' – the men near the doors shuffle towards them like pregnant penguins and the rest of us close up behind. The Number Ones in each stick will be stood in the door with one hand clutching the frame now as the pilot makes final adjustments to line up with the DZ markers. 'Red on!' Red lights glow down at the doors and I try mentally to rehearse the moves my feet should make to the door so that the correct foot will push off from the doorstep. 'Green on! – GO!' – I am aware of dispatchers shouting, 'One! – Two! – Three! . . .' But nothing is happening yet at the back of the stick – there is no room to move forward . . . 'Seven! – Eight! – Nine! . . .' – the outer line of men on my left start to move now and then our line follows on – gaps appear in the line ahead and I stagger forward to catch up – someone ahead stumbles then recovers – 'Nineteen! – Twenty! – Twenty-one! . . .' – men in front are turning left and throwing themselves through the open door – the next few seconds are blurred – 'Twenty-four! – Twenty-five! . . .' – I try not to push against the parachute of the man in front – I glimpse a dispatcher and throw my static line towards him as the man in front disappears and I hurl myself after him into the light.

I am now at the mercy of unseen forces that are pulling my body in all directions at once. I cling to my equipment as if it could provide an anchor as I am thrown around like a puppet under the control of a crazed puppeteer. I see sky, part of a plane, rigging lines, some fields, my feet, there's a parachute below me – I plunge past it, sliding over the edge of the yellow-green material. I look up and see with relief a complete canopy above me, but my rigging lines are twisted together. I am desperate to lower my equipment so I don't land with it on my legs – my thumbs grope for the horns of the hooks that attach it to my harness and force them downwards – the equipment falls away until it reaches the end of the rope that connects it to me. I reach up, pull my risers apart and kick my feet at the air – spinning slowly until the twists disappear. I am happier now – floating downwards with space around me in a sky dotted with nearly four hundred parachutes – just the landing to worry about. There's a pond below me – I drift over it towards a track bordered by ditches. I am drifting backwards, so I quickly pull down my front risers to try and achieve a forward landing – it's not working – 'Head down, shoulders round', – it's a ploughed field – my equipment hits the ground – knees bent and . . . Thump! – I crash awkwardly into the earth, winded but OK. Pull on the lower rigging lines to collapse the wind-inflated 'chute. Throw off the reserve – twist and bang the harness release box with my fist. Look up – others are landing around me. Weapon first – webbing on then bergen. Look for my RV marker – tab towards it.

The drone of aircraft engines continues as successive waves drop their loads. Landrovers drift down over the adjacent heavy drop DZ, each beneath three huge white parachutes – they crash into the earth. Heavily armed and burdened men converge on their various RV markers around the DZ as another six C130s disgorge long lines of men beneath their parachutes. Bloody marvellous! *I love parachuting!*

———— •◆• ————

Darkness would add a new dimension to the military parachuting experience; a night drop added to the drama and increased the risks. On one of our night airborne exercises in West Germany some of the men landed in the Kiel Canal – many drowned.

———— •◆• ————

Training for the Third World War was varied by exercises in Kenya, Cyprus, Canada and Sudan. With time and experience I steadily matured as a soldier. As long as the mighty Soviet Army stayed behind its iron curtain at least the ever-present conflict in Ulster provided a small chance of action, along with a greater chance of being blown to smithereens. My second tour of duty was far from the riots in Belfast down in the rural border areas, attached to 7 RHA, the Para Brigade's airborne artillery, and based in the small market-towns of Bessbrook, Newtonhamilton and the infamously hostile Crossmaglen.

In Newtonhamilton, where we shared a base with a squadron of bored and indifferent Hussars, I was chosen to work in the intelligence cell, which had been neglected there for some time. I was given the key to a room full of files, maps, photographs and old patrol reports – the history of five years of military effort by a dozen or more different regiments that had served at the base. I was a Lance Corporal with no training or experience in military intelligence and I set about my new job with the enthusiasm of a purposeful amateur. My inexperience became evident when I noticed that many intelligence reports contained suspects with the strange Christian name, 'Fnu', which I presumed had a Celtic origin – Fnu Murphy, Fnu McGuire, Fnu Docherty, and so on. I asked an experienced Sergeant about the strange name, and when he had stopped laughing he explained that it meant, 'First name unknown'.

As part of the general information-gathering process the Army had carried out a census of the local population. Patrols would visit houses and ask questions of the occupiers, completing a form that for some obscure reason was known as a 'Farmer's Daughter'. To some people the questions were contentious, particularly when it came to 'Religion?' – Protestants would answer without hesitation and even with a hint of pride, but Roman Catholics would often refuse to say, which was a clear indication that they were, in fact, Catholic. Some people refused to answer any questions, which would invite further military interest in them. A search through all the completed forms on file gave me information to task patrols that would leave the base for a three-day operation, travelling sometimes by helicopter but mostly on foot. I would give patrol commanders a list containing addresses of suspected IRA men to visit and addresses where in the past patrols had recorded that they were given tea and buns, or even a drink of illegally distilled whiskey – 'poteen'. The homes of ex-B Special policemen always proved useful sources of information when included on a patrol itinerary, and I would attach myself to patrols in order to visit them and hear tales of their encounters with the 'enemy'.

Crossmaglen was a different experience – no tea and buns there, and nobody spoke to us unless to mutter an insult. The base was scarred from IRA attacks, and we named it 'The Alamo' – and hung a sign to that effect on the perimeter 'rocket fence'. We would patrol around the small town for a couple of hours or traverse the South Armagh countryside for two or three days at a time, searching for hidden arms caches in hedgerows, stopping and searching cars and always trying to anticipate where the next bomb might be waiting. On one 'Rural Patrol' four unsupported men from the Vigilant Platoon stopped on a road to search cars and were ambushed by 12 IRA men. Two of our men were killed and one seriously wounded – the surviving soldier managed to return fire until the enemy retreated across the border.

There were to be more postings to Northern Ireland for me; my last one came nearly twenty years after my first, and eight years after the Falklands Campaign. On one of my last operations there I commanded a patrol on a mission that would take us to a farmyard in South Armagh that was only yards from the border with 'The South'. I sat by the door of a helicopter that would drop us near our target. With blackened face and hands, and armed 'to the teeth', I was hoping once again for a contact with our elusive and cowardly enemy and an opportunity for some 'payback'. As we gradually ascended we left behind the lights of the towns and headed south into the blackness. I looked down at the retreating signs of civilisation and I was reminded of the boy who had sat on the dark hillside in Cyprus and looked at the village lights below him; the thoughts I had then were echoing now: there were normal people down below – going about their daily lives – watching TV, eating, sleeping, dancing, drinking, making love; but that is as it should be – get on with your lives; I have other business to attend to. I will return to your world occasionally but like some alien visitor I will never really be one of you. This is where I belong. This is my trade. This is what I do best.

The Vigilant Platoons were disbanded in 1977 – the missile was 'first generation' and as such was now obsolete as well as unreliable – it had a habit of turning round in mid-air or flying off on some other course of its own choosing. It was replaced by a more advanced anti-tank weapon called Milan, and I volunteered for a detachment to the School of Infantry in Wiltshire where I commanded a Milan Section for two years, and then, after ten years in the Army and having attained the rank of Sergeant, I decided that I had missed my true vocation as an artist and I left to attend an art college.

I had a parting gift from Irish terrorists just before I was de-mobbed; I was woken in the middle of the night by the bang and blast of an explosion that shook the wooden building in the unfenced training camp in which I lived. Stumbling from my bed I crossed to the door of my room and found that the floor was littered with shards of glass, and flames lit the corridor. I turned back and climbed out of the building through my ground-floor window before moving around to the scene of the explosion. I remember thinking that there might be another bomb – it was an IRA tactic to catch those assisting the injured – when another explosion rocked the building. The second bomb had been left outside my room window; I had stepped over it in the dark without realising it. My room was wrecked and my bed had been blown across the room. There were no serious injuries.

My time as a civilian was a short one – I had made a mistake. I missed my tribe. I was a soldier again less than six months after leaving the Army, and I had rejoined my original Battalion, 3 Para, which at that time was based at Tidworth in Wiltshire.

2. SPEARHEAD

The men thought that victory was chained to my standard. Men who go into battle under the influence of such feelings are next to invincible, and are generally victors before it begins.

John S. Mosby, *War Reminiscences*

———— •◆• ————

Any of 'our' barracks in Montgomery Lines at Aldershot that bore the names of the battle honours, 'Arnhem', 'Rhine', 'Bruneval' and 'Normandy', would have been preferable to Kandahar Barracks in Tidworth, which we thought of as a 'hat' barracks – meant to be occupied by those who could not wear a red beret. Aldershot had been the spiritual home of the Parachute Regiment for many years, although 3 Para had just spent two years in a non-airborne role in Germany. Tidworth Garrison, on the edge of the Salisbury Plain training area, could provide little excitement for off-duty 'Toms' apart from the regular skirmishes with men of the Royal Irish Rangers, who occupied the adjacent barracks.

Not long after my return to 3 Para I found myself training for a third 'tour' (a misleading word) of Northern Ireland – this time to the border areas of Tyrone and Fermanagh in the winter of 1980/81. My time there can be summarised by describing an operation I took part in on New Year's Eve. It was thought by those in command (although as usual not on the basis of any intelligence reports) that the IRA might celebrate the end of the year by firing at one of our permanent vehicle checkpoints near the border. I led a 'multiple' of three four-man patrols to hedgerows on a hillside overlooking the positions on the other side of the border from where the enemy were likely to open fire, and when they did we could join the celebrations by adding fire of our own. It was a cold, wet night and as I lay in soggy earth on the rain-lashed hillside I had a theory of my own: that the IRA would be drinking the night away in a cosy fire-lit bar somewhere. As midnight bells rang out and the rain penetrated several layers of my clothing there came a radio message from the Ops Room: 'Happy New Year everyone!' – promptly followed by a whispered reply from a sodden radio operator, 'Piss Off!'

The incident – or rather the lack of an incident – was typical of most of my service 'across the water'. Long, uncomfortable hours spent hoping for a glimpse of the enemy who never dared risk an open confrontation with us, preferring to take on easier targets including women and children. I had come to regard Irish terrorists as mere gangsters who used their declared objectives to mask their real intent – financial gain and the continuation of the hero-worship they enjoyed in their tribal areas.

The nature of the conflict had changed since 3 Para's first duty there ten years earlier; Army policy had changed and we were adopting a 'low profile'. Any reliable intelligence of what the IRA might be likely to do in our area never reached us, but there would be times when several grid squares of the Ops Room map would be marked 'OOB' – Out of bounds – and we knew that special police units or the SAS would be operating there.

I tended to regard service in Ulster as a necessary break from training for real active service. Professional soldiers, at least in the Parachute Regiment, had a yearning for action that outsiders may find difficult to understand. A soldier who has not been to war is like an apprentice who is never given the chance to work at the actual job. The constant repetition of training, although often realistic and exciting, is still only training. Even so there is much satisfaction to be gained from training to a high standard and carrying out difficult tasks well; but the question remains, 'How would I perform in the real thing?' – and the answer is to be found only in war. The rite of passage, which begins with basic training, is incomplete until the trial of combat is passed.

The lust for combat was stronger in the Parachute Regiment than in most other units. Regimental pride meant an unshakable belief that the Regiment was better than all others, in any army. It could be said that Paras were merely 'brainwashed', and to some extent this may have been true; certainly it is not difficult to convince recruits that they are aspiring to join the best regiment in the best army in the world, because that is what they want to believe. But pride in the past achievements of one's regiment and a determination to maintain high standards are essential ingredients for success in battle. Fortunately the three British Parachute Battalions had survived the sad disbandment of 16 Parachute Brigade in 1976.

In the spring of 1982 the First Battalion of the Parachute Regiment was suffering yet another tour of duty in Northern Ireland, but the other two Battalions were about to complete their apprenticeship and practise their craft for real on an island 8,000 miles away.

In early April I was on detached duty at the School of Infantry in Warminster where I was taking part in the trials of a new thermal imaging unit for the Milan anti-tank weapon. I had just returned from Germany where a stage of the trials had been held, and I had been given some leave before travelling to France to continue the trials. On the morning of Saturday, 3 April I got the first scent of the possibility of action. I woke up in my room in the Sergeants' Mess to the bleating of newborn lambs in the field outside my window. It was a fresh, sunny day. At breakfast I read with surprise of the impertinent invasion of the Falkland Islands the day before by Argentine forces – 'How dare they! So the Falkland Islands are British – where are they?' The invasion had been threatening for a few days, and had been preceded by a group of scrap-metal workers escorted by some military personnel landing on South Georgia (British as well, apparently) and raising the Argentine flag on 19 March. Realising that 3 Para was currently in the role of the Army's 'Spearhead Battalion', a duty that required availability for a short-notice call to action, I decided to go to Tidworth and find out if a call-out seemed imminent.

I drove eastwards across the full length of Salisbury Plain to Kandahar Barracks and entered a hive of activity; equipment and weapons were being made ready for a possible deployment. As I questioned fellow soldiers from the Anti-tank Platoon the Commanding Officer, Colonel Pike, spotted me and asked, 'Are you coming with us, Sergeant Colbeck?'

'Yes sir,' I replied. I could not stop smiling.

3 Para had just received the Milan anti-tank guided weapon, and since I was one of only three men in the Battalion trained in its use I was required to train and lead the remainder of the men who would

form the Milan Section of the Anti-tank Platoon. I considered myself very lucky to be allowed to rejoin 3 Para. Many men were on detachment from the Battalion at the time and almost all, despite their persistent efforts, were refused permission to return. My experience with the Milan system at a time when it was a new weapon to most had made the difference. That same day an intelligence brief, now happily out of date, was to be seen on the Support Company notice board; it concluded, 'As at 31 0800 hrs Z Mar 82 deployment is unlikely.'

I returned to the School of Infantry to collect my military equip-ment and left a note there for the officer in charge of the trials explaining that I would not be going to France and that I had been recalled to 3 Para. I was not sorry to leave the School of Infantry; I had recently been in trouble with the RSM there who had not been impressed by my conduct at a Sergeants' Mess function – I had been banned from the Mess bar indefinitely.

I left the School of Infantry in a patriotic mood and decided to stop in Warminster to buy a Union Jack that I would hoist above the Falkland Islands after our inevitable victory – but there were none for sale. Returning to Tidworth I found that the Battalion had been confined to the local area. The forecast of events board in the Ser-geants' Mess had been altered to read,

> 3 PARA GONE TO WAR
> MAY, JUNE, JULY: SEA CRUISE FALKLAND ISLANDS.

During the next few days, as Argentina rubbed it in by kicking the Royal Marines off South Georgia, we were busy packing existing equipment, unpacking new equipment – and then re-packing again. We were given high priority for new equipment, which included a complete issue of the Army's new range of portable radios, known as 'Clansman'. Quite why the Battalion was not already issued with the necessary equipment and trained in its use, when it was the Army's Spearhead Battalion, I do not know.

Two more Milan firing posts arrived, to add to the existing four. The Anti-tank Platoon also had six Wombat recoilless anti-tank guns. Milan took its name from its French maker's designation, 'Missile,

Infanterie, Leger, ANti-char' (Missile, Infantry, Light, ANti-tank). Wombat, so I was told, stood for 'Weapon Of Magnesium Battalion Anti-Tank' – our primary tank-busting weapons therefore carried the unwarlike names of an Italian city and a cuddly Australian mammal. A Wombat gun was manned by a crew of four and was carried on a Landrover, from which it could be fired, although it was best used dismounted in a defensive emplacement. A gun could be moved by its crew for a short distance on its two wheels, whereas the Milan firing post could be carried by one man, with additional men carrying ammunition for it.

A firing post consisted of an optical sighting system and electronic gadgetry with a launch rail on to which an ammunition tube was loaded. The whole thing sat on a small tripod and turntable. The firer would aim at a tank or other target and press a button to fire the missile, which would receive directional signals from the firing post along a thin wire that unwound from the rear of the missile as it flew. Also at the rear of the missile was a flare that the firing post could detect to confirm the position of the missile relative to the target, and thereby know what corrections to make to its flight direction. The system was incredibly accurate against stationary or moving targets to a range of almost two kilometres, although targets closer than three hundred metres could be difficult to hit because the missile would not at that stage be under full control. The missile carried a HEAT (High Explosive Anti-Tank) warhead that had a shaped charge designed to penetrate armour, although it was effective against other targets, such as defensive emplacements.

The Milan system was limited at night by a dependence on sufficient light for the firer to see his target, a light that could be provided by requesting the fire of illuminating rounds (parachute flares) from either mortars or artillery. The trials I had been working on would provide a solution for the Milan system in the form of a thermal imaging adapter that was designed to detect infra-red light and display it in front of the firing post optical sight; unfortunately the adapter was not in service by the time of the Falklands Campaign.

The Anti-tank Platoon in 3 Para had, in April 1982, a unique Orbat (Order of Battle) consisting of a Platoon of six Wombat crews plus half a platoon (that we called a Section) of six Milan crews – a total, with a Platoon Headquarters, of 49 men. The Platoon was a sub-unit of Support (SP) Company, the home of the Battalion's heavy weapons that as well as the 'Anti-tanks' consisted of an 81mm Mortar Platoon of eight mortars (only six were taken to the Falklands) and a Medium Machine-Gun (MMG) Platoon of six SF (Sustained Fire) machine-guns. The SF gun was the same 7.62mm belt-fed General Purpose Machine-Gun (GPMG) that was carried in each rifle company section, except that it was mounted on a heavy tripod with recoil-buffers, enabling long, accurate bursts of fire. The MMG Platoon at the time had a peacetime role as drummers and buglers in the band – a contentious issue because it was widely believed that an SF machine-gunner should concentrate solely on that specialised task.

There were three rifle companies in 3 Para: A, B and C; each commanded by a Major and consisting of a Company Headquarters and three Rifle Platoons, each of those commanded by an officer (a Lieutenant or a 2nd Lieutenant) with a Platoon Sergeant as his second-in-command. Each rifle platoon consisted of three sections of eight men led by a Corporal. A rifle section was split into a 'rifle group' of six men and a 'gun group' of two men with a GPMG, called 'gimpy' or, simply, 'gun'. The 'gunner' who carried the gun was usually proud of his role as the provider of a formidable supporting firepower to his section in attack or defence. There were 27 such machine-gunners in 3 Para, plus another six in the Sustained Fire role and six with the Wombat crews, a total of 39 guns. 2 Para, which was similarly organised, managed to acquire many more guns before they left England. The GPMG fired the same hard-hitting 7.62mm round as the rifles carried by the majority of soldiers, but the rounds, instead of being held in a 20-round rifle magazine, were linked together with metal clips to form a belt of any length. The Army's standard 'self-loading rifle', or SLR, was a robust and reliable weapon but for close-quarters shooting, particularly at night, it lacked the advantage of an automatic capability – in other words it could only fire single shots, not bursts – unlike the similar but fully automatic rifle used by our Argentine adversaries. A few specialists in the Battalion who carried heavier equipment, such as some of the radio operators, Milan and mortar crews, carried 9mm sub-machine guns (SMG) that were effective only at close range.

In addition to his 'personal weapon' each soldier might carry hand grenades – either high-explosive (HE) fragmentation or white phosphorous (WP) – the latter primarily to lay an instant smokescreen, but a weapon in its own right, bursting in a spray of burning particles of phosphorous. Some men would carry the American shoulder-fired 66mm light anti-tank weapon (LAW), a short range rocket with a similar but smaller HEAT warhead to Milan that was fired from its disposable tube and, like the Milan missile, was effective against non-armoured targets such as bunkers.

Each rifle platoon and each Wombat crew carried an 84mm 'Carl Gustav' medium anti-tank weapon (MAW), similar to the LAW but bigger, heavier and reloadable rather than disposable – an unpopular weapon due to its weight and bulk which were considered to be out of proportion to its effectiveness.

In addition to A, B, C and SP Companies the Battalion had an additional fighting company that was unique to the Parachute Regiment – 'D' or Patrol Company. Operating in four-man patrols in a similar manner to the SAS, they would deploy ahead of the rifle companies in a reconnaissance role, either patrolling towards the enemy or setting up concealed Observation Posts, known as OPs, and reporting back information to Battalion Headquarters by radio.

The total strength of A, B, C, D and SP Companies was around 500 men, who were administered and supported by additional men grouped in Headquarters Company such as pay staff, drivers, cooks, storemen, medics and clerks, all carrying out necessary tasks but referred to by the fighting companies as REMFs, a contemptuous term borrowed from the US Army meaning, 'Rear Echelon Mother-Fuckers'.

The Commanding Officer, Lieutenant-Colonel Hew Pike, had the honour of leading the Battalion at a time when it was about to face its toughest test since the Second World War.

Soldiers of the Parachute Battalions in 1982 were well suited to the type of campaign that was to be fought in the Falklands; we were equipped and trained to operate without reliance on our limited integral transport or on a reliable system of re-supply – as long as we could be delivered to the area of operations by parachute, helicopter or any other means then our feet would do the rest of the work. Most of the other infantry regiments in the British Army were used to travelling to and around the battlefield in tracked or wheeled armoured personnel carriers, supported by heavily armoured tanks and self-propelled guns, along with a vast logistical 'tail'.

The Commandos of the Royal Marines shared a similar ethos of confident self-reliance to that of the Airborne, and between the two units there existed a healthy rivalry mixed with a grudging respect, although each was convinced of its own superiority. The wearers of the two different cap badges had something in common besides the fact that each specialised in either airborne or amphibious warfare – they were specially selected to do so. Whereas an infantry recruit was indoctrinated and trained to perform the tasks required of him, Paras and Marines were in addition the survivors of a series of strenuous and demanding tests, and as such felt confirmed in their belief that they were better soldiers than those who had not passed the same initiation rites. We soon learned in 3 Para that we were destined to deploy as part of 3 Commando Brigade – not as good, we thought, as the old Parachute Brigade, but better than being deployed with an Army infantry brigade.

Colonel Pike addressed his assembled Battalion in the gymnasium at Kandahar Barracks. Deployment was by no means certain at that stage, but the Commanding Officer told us that if we did go it would be aboard the cruise liner, *Canberra*. He also reminded us that diplomatic efforts were being made to resolve the crisis and that as sensible men we should hope that those efforts succeed. If there were any sensible men in the gymnasium that day, then I was not one of them – I would have been bitterly disappointed if there had been a diplomatic solution.

The United Nations had condemned the Argentine invasion and had called for their troops to be withdrawn. Lord Carrington, the Foreign Secretary, resigned – an act that seemed to me at the time to be totally uncalled for, but it has since become clear that the invasion should have been long foreseen and pre-empted; in fact it even appears that our diplomats may have unwittingly encouraged the Argentine military junta by giving the impression that Britain wanted rid of the Falkland Islands. Significant unrest and mass demonstrations in Argentina caused by economic troubles and the 'disappearances' of people created a need to divert the attention of the Argentine people and unite them in a cause – the recovery of *Las Islas Malvinas* would be

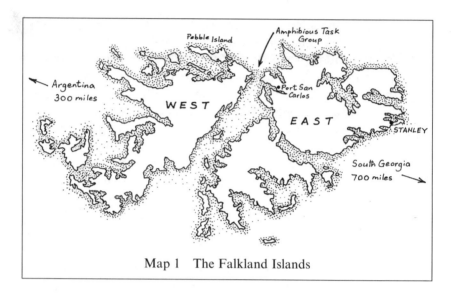

Map 1   The Falkland Islands

ideal for this purpose, and so General Galtieri, fascist dictator and President, had launched his invasion force.

It was only after we had liberated the Falkland Islands that I took any interest in their history. Although an English sea captain made the first recorded landing on the Islands in 1690 and claimed them for the Crown, naming them (no doubt with an eye on his promotion prospects) after Lord Falkland, a British naval official, the first permanent settlement on the Islands was founded by the French, and manned by fishermen from St Malo, which led to the name, 'Iles Malouines' – hence the Spanish, 'Islas Malvinas'. Since that time the 'ownership' and settlement of the Islands was contested by the British, French and Spanish until in 1820 when Argentina, having declared independence from Spain four years earlier, proclaimed sovereignty over the 'Malvinas' and formed the first Argentine settlement there in 1828. The Americans became briefly involved when in 1831 the warship USS *Lexington* destroyed the Argentine settlement in reprisal for the illegal arrest of three US seal-hunting ships. Afraid that the Americans might grab the Islands, the British invaded in 1833 and in a bloodless contest, sent the Argentines back to the mainland, 300 miles to the west. Since that time there has been a continuous British occupation of the Falkland Islands. Our potential adversaries had been taught in primary school that the 'Islas Malvinas' were a part of Argentina.

Ignorant of the full history of the Falkland Islands but having just discovered where they were, I was interested only in the fact that British territory had been invaded, and resolved to help recover it. I saw the media pictures of Royal Marines surrendering as a national humiliation as well as an insult to British armed forces that needed to be avenged. Being a paratrooper I hoped for an airborne assault on to the Falklands but the remoteness of the Islands appeared to make this option a non-starter, although we were ordered to pack our parachuting equipment just in case. 3 Para had made the last British parachute assault on to El Gamil Airfield in Egypt during the Suez crisis in 1956, but since that time there had been a growing debate in the wider Army about the operational need for, and the viability of, parachute troops and there had been an increasing pressure to disband one or more of the Parachute Regiment's three Battalions. After the Falklands Campaign I heard a Para officer comment that our achievements ought to 'keep the sharks out of Parachute Regiment waters for a while'.

Still in Tidworth, the Battalion was placed on 24 hours' notice to move, and men were allowed home on giving the assurance that they could return within that time if recalled. As Al Haig, the US Secretary of State, began his diplomatic peace-seeking efforts and the aircraft carriers *Hermes* and *Invincible* sailed, I spent a couple of drunken nights in The Malet Arms, my favourite pub in the quiet Wiltshire village of Newton Toney, a few miles south of Tidworth, where the landlord sold excellent real ale and had a popular lack of respect for the legal licensing hours. I was usually accompanied on my visits there by Dave McGachan, a Colour Sergeant of the Quartermaster's staff. On our last night before our departure for Southampton docks we approached the pub by our usual route in my car. Driving too quickly into the ford across the village stream I caused the engine to stall, so we abandoned ship, waded ashore and ordered two pints at the bar. The car was still in the stream later that night when the landlord gave Dave and me a lift back to Kandahar Barracks, promising to look after it until my return. The following morning we left Tidworth on the first stage our 8,000-mile journey to the Falklands.

Our equipment was loaded on to Army trucks and we travelled in the relative luxury of civilian coaches – our operational Landrovers had already been driven to the docks and loaded on to a 'Ferry-masters' container ship, the MV *Elk* (where they would remain for the duration of the operation). There had been much speculation about what life aboard *Canberra* would be like. As a young boy I had assembled a plastic model of the ship and I knew that it had a pair of distinctive yellow funnels. Arriving at the movements control centre in Southampton that had been set up in a local Army drill hall, we had our first sight of the Royal Marines who would be sharing the ship with us. The windows of their coaches were hung with slogans such as, 'LOOK OUT ARGIES – HERE COME THE MARINES'.

After a brief halt at the control centre we progressed to the docks where *Canberra* awaited. The Battalion Band greeted us with suitable music, and TV camera crews filmed us unloading our equipment. At last my turn came to climb the gangplank and as I struggled upwards I noticed that many hundreds of cans of beer were being loaded on to the conveyor belt below.

3. VOYAGE

Here where Vespasian's legions struck the sands,
And Cerdic with his Saxons entered in,
And Henry's army leapt afloat to win
Convincing triumphs over neighbour lands,

Vaster battalions press for further strands,
To argue in the selfsame bloody mode
Which this late age of thought, and pact, and code,
Still fails to mend. – Now deckward tramp the bands,

Yellow as autumn leaves, alive as spring;
And as each host draws out upon the sea
Beyond which lies the tragical To-be,
None dubious of the cause, none murmuring,
Wives, sisters, parents, wave white hands and smile,
As if they knew not that they weep the while.

'Embarcation' (Southampton Docks: October 1899); Thomas Hardy,
after observing troops depart for the Boer War

——— •◆• ———

An advance party from the Battalion had been on the ship since the previous day, with the task of allocating accommodation and then acting as guides. We were issued with boarding cards with our cabin numbers on them. 'It's good on there,' I was told as my card was handed to me, 'there are bars everywhere!'

I had been allocated a double-berth cabin with Chris Howard, a Sergeant in charge of the Anti-tank Platoon's 'Wombat' gun section, but when we found the cabin and saw its luxurious interior we agreed that there must have been a mistake – it was surely intended for officers. We decided to keep quiet and began unpacking, hoping that the mistake would be overlooked in the general chaos, but it came as no surprise when the RSM opened the door and told us to move out and make way for two officers. Eventually, after two more moves the confusion was sorted out and I was shown to cabin D56, a single berth that was to be my home for the next forty days.

I was reluctant to unpack, fearing yet another move, but when things seemed to have settled down I realised that I had struck lucky. Most of the other senior ranks had been allocated double berths and corporals and below were in four-berth cabins. My cabin had a private shower and toilet, and was an improvement on the room I had occupied in the Sergeants' Mess in Warminster. 'What a way to go to war!' I thought. The image in my mind when I thought of troopships was one of closely packed hammocks hanging in tiers in every available space; this was so different that it seemed almost farcical.

The feeling of unreality was reinforced when I went to the Pacific Restaurant for my first meal on board. Bow-tied waiters and luxurious décor combined to make the whole situation seem absurd. The Pacific Restaurant had become the dining-room for the officers and senior NCOs, while the Atlantic Restaurant was allocated to the other ranks who did not have the luxury of waiter service and had to queue for their food.

Some of the waiters appeared to be rather less than a hundred per cent heterosexual, and became the inspiration for much ribald comment during our time on board.

I found a P & O Cruises brochure that proclaimed, '*Canberra* is going places in 1982 – Fascinating places that you might never have the chance of seeing again so easily.'

In common with most of the 'embarked force' (over three thousand of us), I found that I easily became disorientated in the numerous stairways and corridors, and it was some time before I learned the shortest route from one place to another.

There was little to do initially, until a training programme was organised, and so I spent most of my time exploring and watching the steady transformation of *Canberra* from cruise liner to troopship. Men in blue overalls were at work everywhere – cutting and welding, measuring and painting. The largest alterations involved the construction of two helicopter landing pads. The Bonito swimming pool had been emptied and steel girders now stood in it to support the 'mid-ships flight deck'. The railings around the games deck were being cut away and lifted by crane to the dockside below; this central landing pad was almost complete when we boarded the ship, but the forward pad was a long way from completion – it was being constructed above the Crow's Nest Bar, which now contained steel roof supports and had become the Officers' Mess. Large sheets of steel were being lifted aboard by crane and then welded together above the bar.

Fuel-intake pipes were being installed to enable 'Replenishment at Sea' from fuel tankers, an operation known as 'RAS'. The Royal Navy, we quickly discovered, used just as many acronyms as the Army.

Our Sergeants' Mess was the spacious and comfortable Meridian Room with a cosy wood-panelled bar, the Century Bar. The remaining bars on the ship were allocated to the junior ranks of the various units. 3 Para used the Alice Springs Bar with its adjoining swimming pool.

Officially, each man was allowed to drink no more than two cans of beer a night – a rule that was almost impossible to enforce, even if there had been a serious effort made to do so. I was becoming familiar with the luxury cruise liner atmosphere and I was only mildly surprised when I found a cocktail waiter in the Century Bar busily shaking drinks for thirsty sergeants.

The six guns of the Wombat section had by now been lifted aboard and lashed to the 'games deck'. Our Milan firing posts and associated equipment were stored in the Island Room where, according to my brochure, we could 'disco dance until the early hours'. Adjoining the Island Room was a children's playroom with cupboards full of games and toys; the room was allocated to a Royal Marines Milan Troop.

The motto of the *Canberra*, displayed on a crest in one of the stairwells was, appropriately, 'For Queen and Country'.

———— •◆• ————

On the day of our departure from Southampton a crowd gathered on the quay and grew steadily in size throughout the day. Alterations to the ship were incomplete but work was to be continued at sea. It grew dark as the entire embarked force assembled at the rails of the ship. We had been ordered to wear our berets and to stand properly, 'at ease'. We also had strict instructions not to wave.

The bands of 3 Para and the Royal Marines were on the quay and took turns to play, and as the 'great white whale' slowly edged away from land the 3 Para band played the inevitable, 'Ride of the Valkyries' by Wagner – our regimental march. Most of our bandsmen were to remain in England, but the drummers/buglers were sailing with us in their alternative role as SF machine-gunners.

As the tugs strained and we made our stately progress towards open water it became evident that far more people had come to observe our departure than we had thought. Thousands of faces and hundreds of Union Jacks stretched all the way along the quay and lined the roads by the sea. As the strains of the band diminished I heard a distinctive male voice in the crowd – 'Give 'em hell!' The deep roar of *Canberra*'s foghorn seemed to reply and the tugs added their horns to the general cacophony. Crowds gave way to cars with noisy horns and flashing headlights and the police entered into the spirit of the occasion by adding blue flashing lights and sirens to the display. People watching from their homes were not to be left out, either, and switched their house lights on and off.

Like so many thousands of men before us we were leaving England to go to war, and the send off was very moving. It was a Friday, 9 April – a week after the Argentine invasion of the Falkland Islands.

The 'teeth arms' of the embarked force consisted mainly of 40 and 42 Commandos of the Royal Marines, 3 Para, and a troop of Royal Horse Guards – the 'Blues and Royals'; the latter were known worldwide in their role as the Queen's Household Cavalry, but with the Task Force performed in their operational role as armoured vehicle crews. The light reconnaissance 'tanks' of the Blues and Royals represented the only armour with the Task Force and were known in general as CVR(T) or 'Combat Vehicle Reconnaissance (Tracked)'. The vehicles were loaded on the *Elk*, one of the many requisitioned merchant ships of the Task Force that were known by the quaint acronym, 'STUFT', or 'Ships Taken Up From Trade'.

Sea King helicopters continued to ferry stores from land to the *Canberra* as we made our way towards the Atlantic with the container ship *Elk* and the RFA (Royal Fleet Auxiliary) *Plumleaf* (a rather odd choice of name I thought, for a ship in support of the Royal Navy).

An Easter Sunday service was held for those inclined to attend, and a routine was established whereby Sunday became a day of rest, and

50

the remaining days of the week were spent carrying out military training. Despite the general unsuitability of ships for the training of land forces we were fortunate that the *Canberra* had more space and better facilities than most of the other ships in the Task Force.

It was quickly discovered that four circuits of the promenade deck were one mile, and we usually began or ended our fitness training with at least ten circuits. Fitness training periods were almost the only time when boots were worn on board, and the promenade deck gradually lost its green paint as the days, and the boots passed by.

I was given the job of training the Battalion to identify different types of AFV (Armoured Fighting Vehicles) and to understand their capabilities. I was given a document produced by the technical intelligence people that listed all the weapons and equipment in use by the Argentine Army. My task was complicated by the fact that the Argentinians had purchased equipment from many sources and their vehicles were a mixture of US, French and German manufacture. Apart from some US-built amphibious landing craft that we knew from news images to have been used in the invasion, we had no idea what other vehicles the enemy had on the Falklands.

I began by making sure that all our soldiers knew how to distinguish our own vehicles, so that they could then be sure that any other types encountered belonged to the enemy and were legitimate targets.

On 12 April the *Canberra Buzz*, a newspaper printed on board, made its first appearance on our breakfast tables. The editor invited contributions from anybody on the ship. It contained jokes and cartoons as well as news, and it also contained 'buzz', hence the title. 'Buzz' is Royal Navy slang for rumour, and rumour is also the soldier's constant companion. I decided to collect a copy of each paper.

From the first edition we learned that Liverpool were '5 points clear at the top' and the 'Latest Buzz' section proclaimed that Argentina was thought to have secretly developed a nuclear weapon. Football results were sacrosanct, and never 'buzz'. The first cartoon showed three rather anxious-looking Argentine soldiers holding their national flag, each with the word 'WOP' on his helmet, cowering from the advance of an angry lion wearing a Union Jack vest. Three lines at the bottom of the first page read:

MET REPORT: GALE FORCE 8, SHOWERS, GOOD VISIBI-
LITY. POSITION AT 120800 A: 100 MILES WEST OF PORTU-
GAL'S COAST ABOUT HALF WAY DOWN. TONIGHT'S FILM
IS: DEATH HUNT.

It was not long before our first 'RAS' took place. There was much
excitement in Royal Navy quarters because this was the first time
since the Second World War that a cruise liner had been refuelled at
sea. The RFA *Plumleaf* drew close and kept pace with us, lines were
fired from the *Canberra*, fuel pipes were connected between the two
ships, and fuel was pumped aboard.

We passed through the Bay of Biscay and the civilian workers who
had finally completed their welding and painting were taken by
helicopter to Gibraltar to catch a flight to England.

It surprised me to learn that some of the Royal Marines who had
resisted the Argentine invasion of East Falkland were on board; one
of them gave an illustrated talk of the experiences of his unit, which
was known as Naval Party 8901. His Airborne audience listened in
polite but cynical silence to his tale of the battle that had raged
around Government House in Port Stanley – after all, the Marines
had not suffered any casualties before surrendering, so just how
severe could the fighting have been? The Marines had done their duty,
of course; hopelessly outnumbered, they had surrendered when
ordered to by the Governor of the Islands – an order that every man
in 3 Para was certain he would have disobeyed – but of course we had
not been there. The action fought by the Marines on South Georgia
appeared to have given the enemy a bloody nose, but again they had
surrendered without loss.

Canberra continued to head south into warmer weather and calmer
seas, and by 16 April we were off the coast of Senegal and
approaching Freetown, Sierra Leone. The *Canberra Buzz* that day
reported that Al Haig, appointed by the USA as a mediator in the
dispute, was back in Buenos Aries with new proposals. A cartoon
showed a two-headed soldier, wearing both a Royal Marine and a
Parachute Regiment badge, inserting a tin of corned beef into an
orifice of an Argentinian general whose trousers were around his
ankles.

The 'Daily Snide' was:

A nasty accident occurred at the Alice Springs swimming pool when 2 paras (Redheads) were accidentally splashed with water. The MO was called and treated them for shock but unfortunately one man still had to have his socks amputated. These are to be buried at sea tomorrow. Keep clear of weather decks Port side 0930.

'Latest Buzz' reported that the Argentine fleet had left harbour the previous night. There was also an obituary for a whale that the ship had collided with during the night; unfortunately this was true.

On 17 April we anchored off Freetown and took on supplies. A British family came to the shore and waved Union Jacks. Word quickly got around the ship that there were women to be seen and it was not long before the decks were full of men. Binoculars were passed around and one of our snipers grinned as he peered through his telescopic rifle sight. Fortunately for these popular and patriotic girls they were too far away to hear the shouted advice from the ship.

The *Buzz* printed the news that Costa Mendez, the Argentine Prime Minister, was optimistic that a solution could be found. My enthusiasm for war had grown even stronger, and I remained optimistic that a solution could not be found. The hopeful anticipation of combat that many of us experienced at the time was, I believe, a necessary part of our mutual preparation for the trials to come. Soldiers who approach warfare with misgivings and trepidation are disadvantaged before the fighting begins.

On Sunday, 18 April, we sailed from Freetown and the first *PARARM Sunday News* appeared. This rival paper to the *Buzz* had a joint Para/Royal Marine editorship, hence the title. It claimed to be more serious than the *Buzz* and devoted over half of its pages to football results – it could not get much more serious than that.

As we journeyed ever southwards the weather became progressively warmer and the physical training correspondingly harder. There seemed to be no limit to the imaginative training methods of the 3 Para PT staff; one of their many brainwaves was to hang climbing ropes beneath the mid-ships flight deck – the hottest place on board when the sun warmed the steel plates above us.

On the morning of 19 April, we had our first sight of an island we were to see for the next 17 days – Ascension.

4. WIDEAWAKE

Literally, *Canberra* is a transport of delight. Capable of wafting you from one romantic place to another, while providing you with all you could want from a holiday in-between the two. Afloat or ashore, the enjoyment, the excitement, is just the same.

P & O Cruises brochure, 1982

————— •◆• —————

Ascension Island lies 900 miles from Africa and 3,700 miles from the Falkland Islands. Barren, volcanic rock rises to the slopes of Green Mountain where the only vegetation is the result of human effort to introduce plants to the Island. For five months of the year Ascension is home to thousands of wideawake terns, and the US airfield on the Island takes its name from them.

Wideawake Airfield was to play a vital role in the operation to recover the Falklands, just as it had done forty years earlier when it provided a link between North America and the North African theatre of war.

Part of the Task Force, including the aircraft carriers HMS *Hermes* and HMS *Invincible*, had already sailed south from the Island before we arrived, but several ships were still there and many more were to join us in the days ahead.

At anchor in the calm waters off Ascension we had a steady platform that enabled us to use the Milan simulator more effectively. The simulator, when linked to a missile firing post, electronically reproduced the effect of a missile in flight, and so adequate training of the firers could take place without the need to fire 'live' missiles. We put two simulators into action and 'fired' at any likely target that could be seen from the ship. Helicopters, landing craft, buildings ashore and parts of other ships were all 'destroyed'.

We had also brought with us a plastic, motorised model tank that we would set in motion on the games deck and use as a target. The press and TV crews became excited when they saw the tank and they filmed it in action, after first insisting on making a miniature Argentine national flag to stick on its turret.

The *Buzz* of 21 April contained this 'Excerpt from the Press':

> The Red Devils of the 3rd Parachute Battalion are preparing to go to war in the Falklands bearing the mark of Satan to strike terror into the hearts of the enemy. By chilling coincidence, the paras aboard Canberra have been given the British Forces Post Office mailing number of 666 – the mark of the Devil mentioned in the Book of Revelations.

Rumour had it that our padre was concerned about the 'chilling coincidence', but we found it rather amusing.

A pen picture of the Commanding Officer also appeared that day:

LT COL H W R Pike, MBE, CO 3 PARA
Lt Col Hew Pike joined 3 PARA as a Platoon Commander in 1963, and was with the Battalion in the Persian Gulf and the Radfan Operation 1964–5. He was later the Intelligence Officer in Guyana (then British Guyana) and Kenya. He served with 1 PARA in Aden and Northern Ireland 1967–70, first with the Patrol Company and then as Adjutant. He commanded 16 Independent Company (Volunteers) 1972–74 and A Company 3 PARA 1978–79 in Northern Ireland and Germany. Jobs away from battalion service have been at HQ AFNORTH Norway (1967), School of Infantry (1970–72), and as Brigade Major, 16 Parachute Brigade (1976–77). He attended the Staff College, Norfolk, Virginia in 1980. His favourite pastime is bird watching, and his favourite colour red. His favourite flavour is cherry and his pet hate is anything green.

I thought that it might be amusing to follow that with an article in similar style about someone nearer the opposite end of the Battalion chain of command. I chose Denzil Connick who was our Platoon Commander's radio operator and well known throughout 3 Para. Denzil, after drinking more than his allocated two cans of beer, was prone to 'opera' singing –

L/CPL CONNICK GSM, 3 PARA
The storeman of Anti-Tank Platoon 3 PARA, LCpl DENZIL CON-

NICK ('Hump' to his friends) was born at a very early age in a Welsh swamp and later found abandoned in a Chepstow telephone booth. He joined the regiment in 1977 after failing an audition for the Covent Garden Opera. Undeterred, he continued to perform in Aldershot at the Globetrotter from where he was transferred to the Queen's Hotel and later ejected to the Royal Exchange. His most recent appointment was as horizontal barman in the Upavon Gliding Club. He is into Gilbert and Sullivan, Double Diamond and Miss Piggy and his favourite food is flies. His pet hate is now the Canberra *Buzz*.

'GSM' (General Service Medal) had in fact been wrongly printed as RSM, which had to be explained to our actual Regimental Sergeant-Major, Lawrie Ashbridge.

Denzil was variously known as 'Hump', 'Frog', or simply 'Taff'. In common with other sub-units in 3 Para, our platoon had its share of men with unusual and often mysterious nicknames – 'Two Heads' Nicholson was another obscure example. Our platoon's second-in-command, Colour Sergeant Steve Knights, was known throughout the Battalion as 'Shakespeare' because of his erudite use of the English language; during his briefings his men would amuse themselves by counting the number of times he said 'fuckin'' or 'shaggin''.

On 23 April, many tons of ammunition were lifted aboard *Canberra* by Sea King helicopters and stored in various parts of the ship. Long 'chain gangs' under the direction of the RSM transferred the heavy containers from the flight deck to spaces down below. Our Milan missiles, already packed in their own transit cases each holding four 'tubes', arrived inside steel boxes that greatly added to their size and weight. The steel boxes were supposed to prevent accidental detonation of the missiles by freak radio waves. The Quartermaster resolved to have the boxes thrown overboard as soon as we could take the missiles out. The same 'radio frequency hazard' also meant that we were not allowed to transport Milan missiles in helicopters or operate radios near them; more rules that would be broken with no adverse effect.

Each night *Canberra* observed 'darken ship' routine. No lights were to be visible from outside the ship, and to this end all windows were blacked out in order to present a more difficult target – the fact that the ship was painted white did not help.

The BBC World Service was our main source of daily news; each cabin contained a radio with one of its four channels tuned to it. Broadcasts over the ship's loudspeaker system, or 'pipes' in naval jargon, cut out the radio channels, often in the middle of an important news item, and this became a constant source of complaint. The hundreds of daily piped messages, frequently of trivial content, continued regardless. One of the four radio channels became 'Radio Canberra' and had a studio manned by volunteers from the troops aboard. These amateur disc-jockeys played requests and made every conceivable mistake as they did so. It was harmless fun to begin with – worth listening to just for a laugh at the DJs' expense, but then traditional rivalry between the Para and Marine units, which had been fostered by various comments from both sides in the *Canberra Buzz*, intensified as the Radio Canberra DJs read requests which were designed to infuriate one of the units. Inevitably the hurt pride began to manifest itself in a physical way, resulting in the occasional fight. The only fight on board that I was witness to, however, was between a 3 Para Sergeant and a member of the press that took place in the Sergeants' Mess over a table of drinks. The off-hand derogatory comment about the Parachute Regiment was soon very much regretted.

Emergency boat drills were a frequent, though necessary, irritation, and I lost count of the times I donned my lifejacket and went to muster stations, mine being the Sergeants' Mess (the bar was closed at these times). The routine of emergency drills was varied on one occasion when we were told that the Mess was 'on fire' and instead we had to squeeze into the cinema. As I waited for the 'all-clear' I began to wonder if they might consider showing an appropriate film such as *The Cruel Sea* or *Titanic*.

We were soon to read in the *Canberra Buzz*, and hear on the radio, the news that two of our Sea King helicopters had attacked an Argentine submarine near South Georgia. On 25 April the *PARARM Sunday News*, true to its avowed seriousness, devoted three of its four pages to sport: Northamptonshire were 253 for 3 against Oxford University (Lamb 102 not out).

South Georgia was recaptured on 25 April by an ad hoc force consisting of SAS, SBS and Marines of 42 Commando; 137 prisoners were taken. So far so good.

———— •◆• ————

On 27 April most of the Battalion was ferried by helicopters to Wideawake Airfield, from where we tabbed across the Island to English Bay, a distance of only around ten miles, but the heat of the mid-day sun made the journey most uncomfortable. The hot tarmac roads caused many blistered feet among us. My Milan section carried firing posts and drill missiles. Every man carried the awkward load in a different way. Each firing post weighed almost 40 and each missile 27 pounds, which in addition to personal equipment and weapons made a heavy burden, although much less than we would carry on the Falklands.

At English Bay, a small cove with a sandy beach, we stood in queues until LCUs (Landing Craft Utility) arrived to carry us back to the *Canberra*. The LCU was the largest of the two types of craft that would be used to transport us from ship to Falklands shore if helicopters were not to be part of the plan (by this stage it was certain that parachuting on to the Falklands was not an option). The LCUs were each capable of carrying over a hundred men.

Even in a calm sea in daylight, boarding *Canberra* from a landing craft, or vice versa, was a difficult manoeuvre; the ship was simply not designed for it. In any kind of sea swell, whether getting on or off the landing craft, you had first to pass your weapon across and then time your jump just right – with a large number of troops a slow process. In perfect conditions at Ascension, I jumped from the rail of the LCU across to the 'hole' in the side of the ship, and two waiting men grabbed my arms and pulled me safely into the Atlantic Restaurant.

Later the same day I decided to buy a diary; they were on sale in the *Canberra* shop, which sold souvenirs and other items such as sunglasses, camera film and T-shirts, just as it would have in more normal times. The diary, which I was to carry throughout my days on the Falklands, measures about three inches by six and is covered in simulated leather coloured blue with 'My Trip' and 'Canberra' embossed in gold on the front. Each page has a space for Date, Place and Weather and below that a few lines on which the voyager could record the events of his or her day. My first entry was on 28 April, when I described the progress so far, and on the following day I made a list of all the ships I could see in the anchorage:

HMS Fearless – *Assault ship and command ship of the landing force.*
Sir Tristram, Sir Geraint, Sir Galahad, Sir Lancelot, Sir Percivale – *LSLs (Landing Ship Logistic).*
Elk – *a roll-on, roll-off ferry.*
The Yorkshireman, The Irishman – *Ocean-going tugs.*
HMS Antelope – *Amazon class frigate.*
RFA Fort Grange – *Fleet Support Ship.*
Uganda – *Cruise ship, now a hospital.*
RFA Pearleaf, British Tamar, Sealift China Sea – *tankers.*

There were also what I thought to be the Ice Patrol Ship, *Endurance*, a salvage vessel and a warship of the Leander class. As I wrote, another tanker, *British Trent* arrived. Including *Canberra* there was a total of 20 ships there that day.

The plan, as we were told at that time, was that the LSLs would head south on 30 April, while we remained at Ascension to await the arrival of other ships from England. We had heard the good news by this time that 2 Para were on their way to join us.

Each evening before dark *Canberra* slipped anchor and sailed all night, returning to the anchorage each morning. The reason for these nocturnal wanderings, so we were told, was to reduce the threat of underwater sabotage. Quite how Argentine frogmen with explosive charges would have been able to get to Ascension and accomplish this daring feat was not clear.

My diary for 29 April reads,

The date for heading South is now said to be 8 May but like most plans made so far it will probably change.

Twelve years in the Army had convinced me that 'Believe it when you see it' was a wise adage.

Date: 30 April 1982, Friday
Place: Several miles from Ascension
1715 hrs: We have been at sea all day doing a RAS with our old friend Plumleaf. *I spent most of the morning teaching vehicle identification. This afternoon there was a lecture on the logistic organisation of the landing force. It is planned to beach 3 of the*

LSLs and the other 2 will ferry stores and ammunition from the support ships. The Elk *will be taken close in and has had a cannon mounted in the bow. The logistics are immense on an operation like this one. Between 8 and 15 tons of stores will be required ashore daily – possibly more if there is heavy ammunition expenditure. The Quartermaster, who gave the lecture, said that there would be a further logistic problem later – the feeding of about 4,000 Argentinian prisoners. The next lecture, however, was about resistance to interrogation in case of capture.*

I am now told that we will go ashore tomorrow to fire MILAN, but only 2 missiles. As I write, Plumleaf *has pulled away and we appear to be heading back to Ascension.*

We took on 2,000 tons of fuel from *Plumleaf* that day. Later that night the World Service reported that the USA had declared support for the UK and had offered logistic aid.

At 7 a.m. on 1 May the Anti-tank Platoon, along with the rest of Support Company, was flown ashore in Sea Kings to Wideawake Airfield where we spent the day firing all our weapons on makeshift shooting ranges in an area known as 'Wideawake Fairs' on the south-west coast of the island.

We began by firing our 'personal weapons' – rifles and sub-machine-guns – to check 'zero', or sight alignment. I was satisfied with the accuracy of my rifle. Afterwards we got down to the even more serious business of firing the support weapons: the 81mm mortars, Wombat anti-tank guns, SF machine-guns and Milan missiles. Seventy-five HESH (High Explosive Squash Head) rounds were fired from the six Wombat guns. Every time a round was fired the blast from the recoilless guns raised a huge cloud of red dust. Various prominent rocks were used as targets and one by one they disintegrated when the warheads exploded on them.

Eventually the Milan Section joined in the fun. From a start point behind the firing point at the base of South Gannet Hill, two teams of two men ran forward and came into action. A missile was fired from each firing post and both flew straight to their targets 1,600 metres away and scored direct hits. This was good for the confidence of the crews, but because we had only been allocated two missiles to fire, it still meant that three of the Milan detachment commanders would go to war in the Falklands without having fired the weapon they were carrying.

I was relieved that both missiles had hit the target because if either had missed the Wombat men would not have allowed us to forget it. A friendly rivalry existed between the two halves of the Anti-tank Platoon; each used a different weapon to destroy tanks, but the Wombat crews were proud of their obsolete guns because of the terrific noise they made when fired. The Milan system had the advantages of being smaller and easier to transport and camouflage, as well as having a greater range.

Shakespeare had saved six Wombat rounds from his allocation and, as a grand finale, ordered them all fired at once. The six guns let rip with a deafening roar that shook the earth under us. I saw one round miss the target and land in the sea but this was strongly denied by all the Wombat crews. It had been a good live-firing day for us but not a good day for the Wideawake Terns that happened to be nesting on the ranges. They were among the first casualties of the war.

Back on board *Canberra* later that day, after we had cleaned our various weapons, we heard the evening news report that Port Stanley Airfield on East Falkland had been bombed by our Vulcan aircraft. This was old news to us – we had passed the very same Vulcan bombers on Ascension that day, and we had been told by the very proud groundcrew who were servicing the returned aircraft. One of the crew tents had 'VULCANS DO IT FOR REAL' chalked on it. The airfield was also home that day to Nimrod and Hercules aircraft and six very new-looking Sea Harriers. The five LSLs had left the anchorage and were now headed southward.

I was surprised to learn that I would be given a sniper as an attachment to my Milan section; a most unusual move and the result of a lack of understanding in the Battalion at the time of the best way to employ these marksmen, which is in pairs. Sniping was a skill that had been neglected for many years, and members of the Battalion shooting team had recently been designated as snipers for this Operation. Corporal Phil Heyward had until recently been a part of the Battalion motor transport section, but was sent with his Lee Enfield rifle to report to me. I learned that his nickname was 'Frut', which stood for 'Fat, Repulsive, Ugly Toad'; I told him that he could be my bodyguard, and decided to call him Phil.

There were some new developments during the week, apart from the recapture of South Georgia – the 200-mile Maritime Exclusion Zone around the Falkland Islands had become a Total Exclusion Zone, meaning that enemy aircraft in the air and on the ground were now legitimate targets. More diplomatic efforts to force an Argentine withdrawal had come to an unsuccessful conclusion. The Toms began to make garrottes from cheese wire supplied by *Canberra*'s kitchen staff.

The weather around the Falklands at the time was described to us as 'appalling', and 'mountainous' seas had been battering the Carrier Battle Group for days. In contrast we were able to sunbathe and enjoy the calm blue seas around Ascension.

On Sunday, 2 May, we heard that fierce air battles had taken place as our Sea Harrier pilots found themselves in dogfights with Mirage aircraft. Two Mirages had been shot down. Part of my diary for that day reads,

I am sat at the bottom of a ramp which leads from the heli-deck above; on it is a trolley attached to a pulley system which has been rigged for moving stretcher casualties. In the Island Room where the MILAN equipment is stored there are packages labelled, 'BAGS HUMAN REMAINS'.

I also noted that the hospital ship *Uganda* had sailed south and another, RFA *Hecla*, had taken its place. The *PARARM Sunday News* ran a competition to find the best lyrics to the tune 'Don't Cry for me Argentina', and informed us that Hull and Widnes had drawn 14–14 in the Rugby League Cup Final.

On Monday, 3 May we heard news of the sinking of the enemy battleship, *General Belgrano*, outside the Exclusion Zone. Also two enemy patrol ships 90 miles inside the zone had been attacked by our helicopters; one sank and the other suffered damage. The war, it seemed, had suddenly become much more real and serious. That night we practised landing craft drills again. It was a bright night with a calm sea and all went well, but it did not take much imagination to see that in bad weather and low visibility it would be slow and dangerous.

The following day I was on duty as the Battalion Orderly Sergeant, a duty that required me to post two lookouts on the 'bridge wings' of the ship, and two at the stern. The lookouts were to report 'suspicious activity', which presumably meant signs of swimmers approaching the ship with explosives.

A television film crew were at work in the Atlantic Restaurant that day – making a film of the Battalion that would be sent home to Tidworth to be watched by the wives. Part of my night duty was to be present in the Alice Springs Bar – the bar used by the 3 Para Toms. The film made that day was being played there and it was suddenly interrupted with the news that HMS *Sheffield* had been sunk. This was surprising news, and I could not help but admire the timing and effectiveness of the Argentinian response to the loss of the *Belgrano*. We all listened to the World Service News at 9 p.m. that night to hear further details about the sinking. We learned that HMS *Sheffield* had been hit by a missile and had been abandoned after catching fire. All men able to abandon ship had been rescued. To add to the bad news, a Sea Harrier had been shot down and the pilot killed.

The Type 21 Frigate, HMS *Antelope* sailed southward and was replaced by another, HMS *Ardent*. We were told that 2 Para would be arriving soon on the MV *Norland* and we would set sail on 6 May, which was good news.

Date: 5 May 1982, Wednesday
Place: Ascension
This morning we experimented with a Scout helicopter to see what MILAN load it could take – the answer is 2 men, 1 firing post and up to 4 missiles, but it's ridiculously cramped.

Apparently, various options for the assault are being worked on, testing different combinations of landing craft and helicopter loads. There should be 18 Sea King and 12 Wessex available as well as Scouts and Gazelles. We all hope that the Battalion will be flown ashore, which is the next best thing to a parachute assault.

Yesterday's news of HMS Sheffield *is the subject of most conversations on board. The few Royal Navy men on board seem to have taken it particularly badly. It must be the first war casualties the Navy have taken for a long time – unlike the Army which has been suffering Northern Ireland casualties for so long now.*

1930 hours: Gave blood this afternoon – several men fainted afterwards. The blood is stored for 5 weeks if not used.

Sail tomorrow 1800 hours with HMS Argonaut *and HMS* Ardent *as escorts and support ships including* Tidespring, Tidepool, Stromness *and* Elk. *The* Atlantic Conveyor *has arrived here and 2 Para are expected tomorrow but will depart later than us. There was discussion on the BBC of the military options – it was said that a landing on West Falkland was most likely. I would have thought that East Falkland is most likely, in the north of the Island within striking distance of Port Stanley which is the key to the Islands.*

It is said that HMS Sheffield *was hit by an Exocet missile fired from a Super Etendard aircraft while the ship was taking part in a shore bombardment. It is rumoured that the lost Harrier flew into the blast of bombs dropped from another Harrier. The* Atlantic Conveyor *has about 20 Harriers on board and some Chinook helicopters.*

On 6 May HMS *Intrepid* arrived, sister ship to HMS *Fearless* and like her carrying eight landing craft. Harriers that had been carried by the *Atlantic Conveyor* flew around in pairs for most of the day. I heard the Task Force numbered 20 warships and 45 merchant ships. The MV *Norland* with 2 Para on board had not yet arrived.

Helicopters were busy that day as usual, constantly moving loads of various sorts from shore to ship or from one ship to another, like bees from flower to hive. The word 'FERRYMASTERS' that was formerly to be seen on the hull of the MV *Elk* in huge white letters had been painted out.

I wrote to the Prime Minister to let her know the strength of feeling I had about the Operation and the determined atmosphere on board, although I doubted that she would have time to read it. PT seemed harder that day than usual and I put this down to giving blood the previous day.

At 5 p.m. that day we left Ascension Island. 'Rule Britannia' was played over the ship's loudspeakers as we slowly moved away from the anchorage with HMS *Argonaut* and HMS *Ardent* as escorts.

That night I noted in my diary that there was a beautiful view from the port side, with a full moon, and that two Sea Harriers were missing in bad weather and they were assumed to have crashed.

5. SOUTHWARD

After all, how often does one get a free Atlantic cruise on the Government?

PARARM Sunday News

———— •◆• ————

Shortly after our departure from Ascension Island, *Canberra* took on more fuel from RFA *Tidepool*. The few ships in our group sailed well dispersed, and made frequent changes of course.

Training continued. Small arms were fired from the stern at bags of rubbish thrown over the side. I wrote a couple of pages on 'Anti-Armour Operations at Company Level' which was printed and distributed to the three rifle companies. It ended with a little propaganda – 'Anti-Armour warfare requires great determination and initiative – it is very much a David and Goliath confrontation; but you are a very well trained and equipped David.' I continued to teach men how to identify the various types of enemy tanks and other armoured vehicles. We had no further information about the types and numbers of vehicles the enemy were using. In fact all the lessons I gave on the many types of enemy vehicles were to prove a waste of time – the only enemy armoured vehicles we encountered were parked in Port Stanley, and we did not see them until the war was over. But the lessons kept us busy. Weapon training, first-aid and other training also continued, but we had exhausted most subjects. We had reached a stage where we had trained to a peak in most subjects and further repetition would have been boring and counter-productive. We were ready for what lay ahead and just needed to be told what our commanders expected us to do. So we began to 'cross-train' – the specialists in each weapon system taught their skills to each other. I taught the Wombat and Mortar crews how to load and fire Milan missiles.

We were issued with a Spanish language sheet that contained such useful phrases as:

How many troops are there in ...?
QUANTOS SOLDADOS HAY AQUI?
Where is your leader?
DONDE ES SU JEFE?

I learned only one phrase from the list: 'ARRIBA LAS MANOS!' (hands up!).

———— •◆• ————

The *Canberra Buzz* fell silent on 8 May, and the newspaper was superseded by the *Canberra News*. The *Buzz* had been silenced because it was thought that the inter-unit sniping it contained was bad for morale. The 'Daily Snides' column had contained this fine example:

An Arab Sheikh lay dying. His 3 sons stood around his bed. He asked them what they would like from him before he died:
1st SON   A plane.
FATHER   I shall buy you a fleet of supersonic jets my boy.
2nd SON   A boat.
FATHER   I'll buy you a fleet of ships my boy.
3rd AND YOUNGEST SON
                 I want a cowboy outfit, dad.
FATHER   Son, you shall have 3 PARA.

The *Canberra News* was allowed to print on the assurance that it would not print such 'snides'. Dave McGachen and I responded to the request for 'Newshounds'. Dave wrote under the name of 'Scoop', and I became 'Clark Kent'.

Water on *Canberra* began to be rationed, and mail delivery and collection became much less frequent. The ship had taken on board many sacks of mail from would-be pen friends. It became a popular sport in 3 Para to choose a letter containing a photograph of an unattractive girl and reply to it in the name of someone else in the

Battalion. Some of the most amusing letters and interesting photographs, including some naked poses, were stuck on corridor walls.

I heard that someone in 3 Para had taken white feathers from his pillow and sent them to 1 Para, the only battalion of the Parachute Regiment who would not be going to the Falklands; they were serving in Northern Ireland.

On 9 May the *PARARM Sunday News* began a scoreboard of the losses in the match so far:

BRITAIN	ARGENTINA
1 × Sea King	1 × Submarine
3 × Sea Harriers	1 × Cruiser 14,000 tons *Gen. Belgrano*
1 × Type 42 HMS *Sheffield*	1 × Patrol boat + 1 damaged
	2 × Mirages and 1 possible
	1 × Canberra and 1 possible
	1 × Airfield and 1 Island

Interestingly, there was no mention of any human casualties. The airfield referred to was Stanley Airfield, assumed to have been put out of action by the Vulcan bombing raid, but in fact Argentine aircraft were able to land and take off from it right up until the end of the war.

We also read that Peter Shilton had been put on the transfer list and Glen Hoddle (Spurs) would be out of action for at least two weeks.

On 9 May an inter-unit sports day was held – it was won by 42 Commando, with 3 Para second, 40 Commando third and the fourth place was shared by teams from Minor Units and the Ship's Company. 3 Para were easy winners of the 10,000 metres race, but the hero of the day was Laundryman Frank Taylor of the Ship's Company, who finished in second place.

One day we were treated to a demonstration firing of HMS *Ardent*'s 4.5 inch gun. The frigate sailed close to *Canberra* and fired several rounds that exploded in the sea. Afterwards some of *Ardent*'s crew came on deck to wave to us.

Most of us in 3 Para were ignorant of the specialist work of Naval Gunfire Observers (NGFO) whose job it was to direct the fire of the guns at sea from a position on land. A NGFO Party of four men gave a presentation to 3 Para in the cinema, explaining the jobs each of them was responsible for. They also described their training and selection, which included the Airborne P Company tests as well as the Royal Marine Commando Course. When they asked for questions afterwards I rather cruelly asked if they had found the Commando Course a good build-up for P Company, knowing that it would raise a laugh, which it did. I received the answer I expected – the Commando Course was in fact the most demanding of the two.

On 11 May, the officers and senior ranks were treated to a seven-course meal with wine. The printed menu featured a picture of Southampton waterfront in the early nineteenth century.

———— •◆• ————

All these distractions hid a growing tension and sense of anticipation as we sailed further south and the weather became predictably worse. My diary contains the following entry for 11 May:

> *I've been told today of the plan for landing and I'm not particularly pleased about it. 3 PARA are going to land by landing craft at a settlement on the West side of East Falkland called Port San Carlos. We are to take up a defensive position there. I think we should be going straight for the Port Stanley defences after a heavy bombardment. We are told that the Argentine troops are poorly supplied and morale is low – mainly because of bad weather and the occasional bombardment. By going into defence we are also going to suffer from the effects of the weather and become vulnerable to air attack. We will still have to attack Port Stanley and we will be far from the peak condition we are in now. I think we should be attacking from the outset and taking out their best units first. Casualties would be high but with this plan they may be higher in the long run.*

I smile when I read that now; it is typical of the Airborne soldiers' attitude to warfare to want to get to grips with the enemy as soon as possible (*'being paratroopers, they immediately attacked'*).

The feeling that we should attack the enemy defences around Stanley was common among most of the men I spoke to, but of course it is easy to criticise a plan made by someone else, especially when one is ignorant of all the factors involved; but despite all the doubts we had about the various orders we were given during the Campaign, there was never any hesitation shown when it came to carrying them out. The wisdom behind a plan may have been in question, but just as a paratrooper might have doubts about throwing himself through the open door of an aircraft, when the green light comes on there is no turning back. It is natural to be critical of the people who make decisions that will determine your future (or lack of one), and in this respect military leaders are like politicians, but a soldier cannot vote for his officers, though he may wish that he could.

There was to be no move ashore before 16 May. Ammunition was to be issued to us 48 hours in advance of the landings, but grenades would not be made available until just before we boarded the landing craft.

I usually walked on deck after the evening meal, and I would join one of the small groups gathered at the rail and watch the other ships as the sun fell towards the horizon. We were then part of a convoy of 11 ships. The MV *Norland*, usually a North Sea Ferry, had joined us carrying 2 Para and some medical and artillery units. HMS *Fearless* and HMS *Intrepid* could usually be seen. The ships were constantly flashing Morse Code light signals to each other, which somehow seemed to add a feeling of unity and urgency to the widely spread convoy. Dave McGachen had been in the Battalion Signals Platoon and could decipher the flashing lights. One evening he called out the letters to me as a warship winked in our direction. I wrote the letters down and when we had formed them into words we were disappointed to have received only a routine message about rations.

As I continued my diary on 12 May at 4 p.m., RFA *Stromness* was on our starboard side and Sea Kings were 'cross-decking' stores from her to *Canberra*. Most of the nets carried beneath the helicopters contained beer and as I watched a crate fell into the sea. Evidently our supplies were running low.

Date: *13 May 1982, Thursday*
Place: *South Atlantic*
Weather: *Colder but bright clear sky*
This morning we were 1,000 miles east of Buenos Aries. Wrote a short history of 3 PARA for the newspaper today. Some of the BFBS [British Forces Broadcasting Service] radio broadcasts are

being jammed by Argentina. Latest rumour is that we are landing on the 20th. 3 enemy aircraft have been shot down west of the Islands – 12 aircraft took part in an attack on our ships. There has been more talk of a diplomatic solution and a mutual withdrawal with UN intervention. I do not believe for one minute that we will turn around now – we must at least land and raise the flag. Public opinion at home will not stand for anything less. Another RAS yesterday with Tidepool. *Apparently many people at home are sending gifts to the Task Force – knitted gloves and hats, etc., and more beer has been donated by another brewery – the last got as far as Ascension and the RAF drank it all.*

Appearing in the *Canberra News* the same day was:

Alphabet Sentence Practising the word 'Fortunately'
An Argentinian pilot had just taken off from Buenos Aries when he suffered engine trouble:
Fortunately he was heading for a mountain face.
Unfortunately he was able to jump out.
Fortunately his chute didn't open.
Unfortunately there was a haystack below him.
Fortunately there was a pitchfork concealed underneath.
Unfortunately he missed the hay as well . . .

In my diary the next days:

Date: 14 May 1982, Friday
Place: Further south
Weather: Poor visibility, heavy sea
I watched an albatross at the stern this morning. It was gliding effortlessly behind us on its huge wings.
   Equipment is packed now. Mine weighs a lot even before ammunition and rations have been issued. I am due to land with B Coy – but I will be surprised if that doesn't change.
   5 weeks from Southampton.

Date: 15 May 1982, Saturday
Place: 45 degrees 3 minutes South, 58 degrees 56 minutes
             West

Weather: Bright, showery, heavy seas
Now in 'Roaring Forties'. Temperature 53 degrees F. We are now
824 miles from the Falklands. There was a Force 7 gale during the
night. Tidepool *has turned North, to re-fuel from* British Dart.
Battle preparation is now in full swing. We are now gluing together
maps of the landing area – Port San Carlos is at the junction of 4
maps.

1800 hours: We are now 3 hours behind GMT and 4 behind
Britain, but we will be working on ZULU time for the operation.
We are to land about 2 hours before dawn. Special Forces are
ashore and will signal us all clear. The landing craft run-in will take
about half an hour. I hope the sea isn't as rough as it is at this
moment – we are rocking about so much that all the woodwork is
creaking.

Once ashore we are going to conduct 'offensive operations' –
after the defensive position is consolidated – which isn't going to be
easy with the bulk of the enemy 50 miles away.

I shouldn't take this diary with me but I'll consider it – or start a
new one.

On Friday a raid was carried out on an ammunition dump and
some aircraft were destroyed – there were only 2 minor British
casualties.

I've just been down to the rear of D Deck – E Deck is awash. It's
pitch black on deck and we are being tossed around more than I
would have thought possible for a ship of this size. We are fortunate
to be on this ship – the LSLs and other, smaller ships must be
suffering much more.

On 16 May we were part of a fleet of 18 ships. There had been another
Force 7 gale during the night but I had slept well. We were told 'No
move ashore before 18 May.'

The *PARARM Sunday News* adjusted the scoreboard:

BRITAIN	ARGENTINA
2 × Sea Kings	1 × Submarine
3 × Sea Harriers	1 × Corvette hit by a Carl Gustav
1 × Type 42 HMS *Sheffield*	1 × Cruiser 14,000 tons *Gen. Belgrano*
	1 × Patrol boat and 1 damaged

2 × Mirages and 1 possible
5 × Sea Hawks
1 Aeritalia or Hercules
2 × Airfields
1 × Minelayer/Tanker
1 × Ammo dump
2 × Troop-carrying helicopters

Most of the new 'score' was the result of the Pebble Island raid by the SAS. There were no sports results but we learned that Ralph Reader, the founder of the Gang Show, had died aged 78. Inspired as usual by Corporal 'Blandy' Bland of A Company, a group of notorious performers from the Battalion had planned a Gang Show of their own; set to consist of a number of comedy sketches and to take place in the cinema in front of the rest of 3 Para. The show had the full support of the RSM but the Royal Navy commander of the embarked force decreed that it could not go ahead; evidently he was of the opinion that in the circumstances the show would be too flippant. He had no understanding of the character of British soldiers. One of Tommy Atkins's great strengths is his sense of humour, which is rarely absent even in the most trying situations, and any attempt to stifle it will usually be a mistake. The cancellation of the show was a great disappointment to all.

During the afternoon of 16 May we were issued with rations for the first three days of the land operation, and the next day the company commanders held their 'orders groups', or 'O groups' (briefings to their sub-unit commanders).

My Milan Section was to be split between B and C Companies. Two firing post crews (one Milan detachment) under the command of Corporal Mathews would be attached to C Company, and I would take the remaining four crews with B Company. I therefore attended the 'O' group of the Officer Commanding B Company, Major Mike Argue.

The use of O groups was part of 'Battle Procedure', an effective system that was designed to ensure that orders were passed from the highest level to the lowest. Our Commanding Officer, Colonel Pike, along with the COs of 2 Para and the Commandos, would attend the O Group of the Brigade Commander of 3 Commando Brigade, Brigadier Thompson, where he would be briefed on the Brigade plan and

3 Para's part in it. The CO would then return to his Battalion and make his plan to achieve the given mission before summoning his O Group at which he would pass on his orders to his company commanders, together with representatives from any attached armour, artillery, and so on. A similar briefing would then take place at company level after the company commanders had made their plan. I was therefore one of the links in a long chain, and after receiving my orders from Major Argue I would extract the relevant information to pass on to my Milan detachments.

The B Company O Group took place in one of the larger cabins. During the orders I learned that B Company were to be the first company ashore from 3 Para, transported in the smaller landing craft, LCVPs. Their task was to secure a bridgehead until A Company passed through them to the Port San Carlos Settlement, then to move to Windy Gap, a high feature to the northeast of the Settlement, and set up a defensive position there (see Map 2, p. 87). My Milan detachments would be a part of that defensive position. I asked how the Milan crews would get ashore, and Major Argue told me that we would be taken by helicopter, but he had no details. This was most unsatisfactory, as I should have left the O Group with all the necessary details for my part in the plan. When a board that held the briefing map toppled forward on to Major Argue's head, I hoped that it was not a bad omen.

I went in search of Major Dennison, the Support Company Commander, to ask if he had any details on transport ashore for us; he told me that we would be taken ashore with C Company in the larger landing craft, and I would RV with B Company later. I then returned to Major Argue and arranged to meet him at an agreed point that we selected on the map.

———— •◆• ————

That day we were 280 miles east of Port Stanley, and our fleet of ships was growing in number. We were shown some slides of Port San Carlos Settlement and told that H-Hour would be during the morning of 21 May. It was still planned to get us ashore two hours before dawn.

Canberra refuelled again from *Tidespring*.

Dave McGachen and I had been writing articles for the *Canberra News* that had not been included by the editor, so we decided to print one edition only of a newspaper for 3 Para only, which we would call *Green Lanyard*, the name of a Battalion publication of former times (after the coloured lanyard we wore on our left shoulder in peacetime). When we asked for a supply of paper we were told there was a shortage, and therefore our plan was impossible. Undeterred, we went in search of Tony 'Dog-End' Dunn of B Company who, like all good Colour Sergeants, had some useful contacts (he had, for example, found out from a crewman that all the furniture on the ship would be an insurance write-off, and he was considering packing some of the swivel chairs in the Sergeants' Mess to take home). Secretively, Dog-End led us to a lift that we had not noticed before (all lifts were out of bounds to the embarked force), and in it we descended, emerging into an Aladdin's Cave that contained, among many interesting items, several boxes of printing paper. In this way we acquired a sufficient stock of paper to enable *Green Lanyard* to go to print.

On 18 May I briefed the 13 men who were to be under my command and attached to B Company, consisting of four Milan crews each of three men, plus our sniper. I found a quiet corner of the Pacific Restaurant and the men sat around my map boards at tables with clean white tablecloths. I still have my notes for the orders, which I left behind in a suitcase on *Canberra*:

ORDERS

1. SEATING [showing arrangement of men relative to briefing map]
Map & diagram [of operational area]
74D 74C 74G 74B 74A
[Radio call-signs for each firing post commander and the sniper (74G).
My call-sign was 74]

2. INTRODUCTION
The Op is called Op SUTTON and is scheduled to take place on Fri 21 May before first light. Re-briefing will take place on Thu 20.

3. GROUND
a. *(explain map*[†]*) FALKLAND SOUND, SAN CARLOS WATER. Note in particular PORT SAN CARLOS, water 80 feet deep (compare map with diagram area).*

[†] The reader should refer to Map 2, p. 87.

74

b. *(explain diagram) Drawn to scale – grid lines marked as shown.*
Green lines represent contours (describe shape of ground).
Blue lines – coast and main streams.
Straight black lines are fences – may have changed since 1956 when map was printed.
Dotted black lines are main tracks – there may be more.
Red lines and black letters are positions for phase 3 – ignore for now. The marker indicates the proposed landing point.
c. *Areas of note – SETTLEMENT – population 30 + , AIRSTRIP – 650 feet long, SAND BEACH, SECONDARY BEACH and SETTLE-MENT ROCKS – note in particular WINDY GAP.*
d. *Scale. Beach to WINDY GAP = 5000 metres.*
e. *North. (Indicate)*
f. *Ground from SAND BEACH to WINDY GAP – flat initially then growing steeper with ridge on left hand side – track contours up to saddle crossing a few streams on the way.*
g. *Ground as seen from WINDY GAP (Saddle)*
WEST – rising to SETTLEMENT ROCKS
NORTH–WEST – dropping to FISHERMAN'S VALLEY
NORTH – looking across valley to hills 1600 metres distant.
NORTH–EAST – dropping to GULLET VALLEY
EAST – rising from saddle to a high ridge – CERRO MONTEVIDEO – 5000 metres distant.
SOUTH – falling steeply to PORT SAN CARLOS, rising other side.
WEST–SOUTH-WEST – PORT SAN CARLOS SETTLEMENT, AIRSTRIP, and west of that, SAND BEACH.
In general, probably a lot of dead ground, especially NORTH and NORTH-EAST.
h. *Night moves. Plan on 1 km per hour recommended by Special Forces ashore.*

4. SITUATION

a. **Enemy Forces**. *You already know about the general enemy locations and organisations. I'll just remind you of enemy forces which are a threat to our area of operations. In the whole area of Brigade operations in the very worst case there is an infantry regiment (Battalion equivalent). The area of operations is out of range of present enemy artillery. GOOSE GREEN/DARWIN area (which has an airstrip) based the following: A strategic reserve consisting of 12 Infantry Regiment and 601 Commando thought to consist of no more than 500. They have a heli-lift capability.*

FANNING HEAD. Possibly an enemy company – probably only a platoon – dug in (10 km NW of Port San Carlos).
PORT SAN CARLOS. Has been visited by enemy helicopter patrols – if it is occupied by enemy they are no more than platoon strength.
Armour *is no threat in this area.*
Aircraft *are a major threat. Milan might be used with some success against helicopters. Positive identification as enemy is essential – especially of Chinook, Puma, Alhouette, Huey.*
Dress *– American style fatigues and helmets. Special Forces – cowboy dress – possibly camouflaged fatigues. Possibly white shell dressing on helmets. Marines wear West German style helmet.*
Weapons *– Good small arms, grenades and mines. Some homemade mines used on South Georgia and also responsible for injuries on Pebble Island – command detonated.*
Morale *– Very bad at Stanley, they are dug in but not camouflaged. No discipline and lack of effective leadership. Many cases of dysentery and exposure deaths. During the raid on Pebble Island by the SAS, counterattack by Argentinian marines retreated after their officer was shot.*
Tactics *– in our area the main risk is a heliborne counterattack by ground forces and attack by FGA aircraft.*

b. **Friendly Forces**. *SAS and SBS have been on the Islands in a recce role for some time. Dress of special forces includes a white headband to aid identification.*
The Brigade is to land and secure PORT SAN CARLOS and SAN CARLOS WATER and use it as a base for future offensive operations. 40 Cdo and 2 PARA – SAN CARLOS; 45 Cdo – AJAX; 3 PARA – PORT SAN CARLOS; 42 Cdo – Reserve.

Battalion Plan

The Battalion is to land by sea, secure a beachhead (B Coy), take the Settlement (A Coy) and secure the area of Settlement Rocks (C Coy) – thereafter to form a defensive position based on PORT SAN CARLOS settlement. The Battalion will be supported by naval gunfire, artillery and mortar fire, Blowpipe, Rapier, 4 armoured vehicles and a troop from 9 Sqn RE. Air support consists of 8 Sea King, 4 Wessex (1 gunship), 4 Gazelle (rockets) and Scout (ATGW).

Company Plan

B Company is to land by sea and deploy to defend a bridgehead before establishing a defensive position in the area of WINDY GAP. The Company is supported by artillery, mortar, MMG, Milan, 1 Blowpipe Det, 1 Rapier Det, 1 Scimitar, 1 Scorpion and Cpl Heyward!

Atts and Dets. Attached we have Cpl Heyward as a sniper. Detached are call signs 74E and 74F to C Company.

5. MISSION
We are to land and make contact with B Company and move with them to set up a defensive position in the WINDY GAP area (repeat).

6. EXECUTION
   a. General Outline – a 3 Phase operation.

      Phase 1: Sea landing by LCU and establish contact with B Company.

      Phase 2: Move by foot with B Company to a Coy RV southwest of the WINDY GAP area.

      Phase 3: Recce and occupation of defensive position WINDY GAP area.

   b. Detailed Tasks – Phase 3

      74A – To take up a position indicated by me in the area of GR 645931 with primary arc NE–E–SE, secondary arc SW–W (possibly with a second position). Your position will probably be within 4 Platoon area.

      74B – To take up a position indicated by me in the area of GR 644932 with an arc NE–N. Probably within 4 Platoon area.

      74C/D – To take up a position indicated by me in the area of GR 638933 with an arc NE–N–NW. Probably within 5 Platoon area.

      74G (Cpl Heyward) – To be located with me in a central position of observation between the 2 Detachments.

      Note: *Also based within the Coy position will be 1 Scimitar and 1 Scorpion. Later, after the heli-lift – 1 Rapier, 2 Wombat (72A, 72B) in 4 Platoon area covering tracks. Each platoon will have a 4 man OP forward.*

   c. Co-ordinating Instructions

      No timings yet – a pre-dawn operation initially becoming light before Phase 3 and possibly before Phase 2.

      30 minutes from ship to landing point – hugging coast or mid-water if enemy on land a danger. We will be 10 minutes behind B Company.

      Before the start of the Op a special forces troop will land to the north and take out the enemy on FANNING HEAD. This force will then split – part of it will recce our landing beach.

      We will be in LCU 1603B (C Coy on left, A Coy on right)

      Lights on the beach will at first be special forces – then only one red flashing light.

      On disembarking move in single file to RV with B Coy HQ at stream junction GR 607927 – distance 700 m. As we move up the beach mortars will be setting up on our left. Beware of mortar rounds dumped on the beach by rifle coys. Keep closed up.

      There may be a long wait at the beach before Phase 2 begins.

*Order of march for Phase 2: 5 Platoon, Coy HQ, Milan, 6 Platoon, 4
Platoon. Our order of march will be myself, Cpl Heyward, 1 Det, 2 Det.
There is a track to the Coy RV at GR 642933. The Recce Group will go
forward from there to site weapons. We will then move into positions –
don't start digging until final confirmation of arcs.*

d. *Priority of work*

1. *Concealment of temporary positions.*

2. *Range card/fire trench.*

3. *Ammo bay.*

4. *Shelter bay.*

5. *Overhead protection.*

6. *Final camouflage.*

Stick to the Coy track plan.

Night Visibility Plan – illumination authorised by Bn HQ.

Permission to open fire will come from Coy HQ.

Defence stores are unlikely to arrive at the position before the night of D + 1.

Patrols will initially be clearance and OP, then offensive.

Coy HQ GR 645930 to the rear of 4 Platoon.

(Cover Actions On) ['Actions on' are contingency plans for eventualities
such as encountering the enemy at any stage]

*Summary of Execution (outline of Bn + Coy plans from beach to WINDY
GAP).*

7. SERVICE SUPPORT

Most of this has already been covered – kit, ammo, etc.

a. *Draw ammo tomorrow morning – prepare MILAN ammo later.*

b. *More MILAN ammo will be brought to the defensive positions later
(maximum 6 per post?).*

c. *You can wear a waterproof in the LCU – remove them at beachhead.*

d. *Medical – each man one morphine. All casualties are to be left with rifle
upended. Dead are to have one ID disc hung from the rifle – keep 1 for
Coy HQ. All casualties will be taken later to Coy HQ and then to the
RAP. Heli casevac will be to hospital ship – if flying impossible then by
boat. The RAP will be in the Settlement Bunkhouse.*

e. *Sea kit bags may arrive ashore after 5 days.*

f. *You must retain the ability to manpack MILAN throughout the defence.*

g. *POW to Coy HQ and from there to SAND BAY.*

h. *Rations as issued – 1 day on man, 2 days in bergen.*

i. *4 batteries per radio to be carried – remainder in bergens.*

j. *Bergens will be brought to the defensive position when transport is
available.*

8. COMMAND AND SIGNALS

a. Chain of command – myself then senior Cpl downwards.

b. Signals instruction and *MAPCO* will be given out later. No *SLIDEX*, no *VOCAB*. Always use 6-figure *MAPCO*.

c. Additional signals:

GREEN ONE	= SAND BAY
GREEN TWO	= ALTERNATIVE BEACH
MUSKETEER	= START PHASE 3
SCABBARD	= SETTLEMENT SECURE (A Coy)
DRY BONE	= C COY AT SETTLEMENT ROCKS
MIRROR IMAGE	= A + C Coys DIVERT TO GREEN TWO
ROCKY LANCE	= WHOLE FORCE DIVERT TO GREEN TWO
SILVER FOX	= WINDY GAP SECURE (B Coy)

d. Telephone line will be laid from Coy HQ.

e. Short whistle blasts = AIR ATTACK
   Long whistle blasts = GROUND ATTACK
   1 × Long whistle blast = ALL CLEAR

f. Radio silence until contact.

g. Take only necessary documents ashore – keep signals instructions secure (with signaller at all times).

h. Password: Not issued yet. [This was in fact two words, a challenge and a reply – long since forgotten]

i. Synchronise watches. Questions.

What may seem like a complicated set of instructions was in fact quite easily understood by those who took part; similar tasks had been practised by the Battalion on exercises many times before. The main difference on this occasion, apart from the real enemy threat, was the part where we were expected to float in a steel tub for half an hour, but the cover of darkness would provide some security. Operation Sutton did not go quite as planned, but in war things rarely do.

'Musketeer', the codeword for the start of Phase 3, had also been the codeword for 3 Para's Suez Operation 26 years earlier.

Later that day, 18 May, after I had given my orders and made sure that they were fully understood by my men, I was working with Dave McGachen on articles for the *Green Lanyard*, which was almost ready to be printed, when we were interrupted with the news that the Battalion was to move to HMS *Intrepid* 'at first light' the next day. 40

Commando was to move to HMS *Fearless*. A hectic period followed as ammunition was quickly issued and we repacked our equipment. The corridors echoed with the sounds of shouted instructions and of metal ammunition containers being broken open. Men ran back and forth heavily laden. A man rushed past me with several belts of machine-gun ammunition draped over his shoulders and rifle ammunition cradled in his arms, shouting, 'We're all doomed!' The sudden decision to disperse the amphibious units was rumoured to be the result of a broadcast by the BBC that stated that *Canberra* had joined the assault fleet with 2,000 troops on board. Control of the media was in general very tight during the Campaign, and was made easier by the remoteness of the Falkland Islands and the control of communications by the services, but the news that so many troops were on a defenceless ship so close to the Islands put us at greater risk. There will always be a conflict between the military need for secrecy and the media need for vivid material.

After I had hurriedly issued ammunition to my men and loaded and packed my own I was told that my Milan Section was not required to move from *Canberra* with the rest of the Battalion after all, presumably because our bulky Milan missiles were still aboard the ship and would be difficult to move. But on the morning of 19 May I was told that we would in fact move with the rest of the 3 Para assault force to *Intrepid*.

Before we said goodbye to the 'Great White Whale', Colonel Pike assembled the Battalion and our attached troops in the Meridian Lounge to speak to us all, as commanders tend to do on such occasions (and there was unlikely to be space on *Intrepid* to do the same). Among other things, the CO urged us not to delay the Operation by stopping to help casualties until our objectives were secure (immediate aid to the wounded had become a feature of our contacts in Northern Ireland). After the talk we returned to our cabins for the last time and waited for a call on the pipes to proceed to the landing craft loading point.

While I waited I read a book (the title of which has long since slipped from memory) from the ship's library, and when the call came to move I abandoned it, unfinished, on my bed. Struggling under my heavy load I joined the procession of troops to E deck and the Atlantic Restaurant. We carried all the weapons, ammunition and equipment that we would be taking ashore with us, apart from Milan missiles, mortar bombs and grenades, which had already been cross-decked by Sea Kings. Our bergens were left behind on *Canberra* and would, if all went well, be moved ashore some time after we had landed. Bergens were each identifiable by a company colour and individual number that we had painted on the back, and contained a sleeping bag, spare clothing, two days' rations and other items such as radio batteries, washing and shaving kit and so on. Also packed in our bergens were our gas masks, as the threat of chemical warfare was not regarded as serious enough to warrant carrying them ashore with us, although we had been told that the Argentines had old supplies of mustard gas. Our sea kitbags also remained on *Canberra*, and contained luxuries such as spare boots, clothing and books, and was known as 'follow-up kit'.

With some difficulty we managed to climb into the landing craft as it bobbed around in the sea below us, and when we were all aboard the crew cast-off and turned the LCU towards the waiting *Intrepid*. It was a grey day with some mist but as we forged through the rough sea we were able to see the aircraft carrier HMS *Hermes*, and I counted six Harriers taking off from her in quick succession, presumably to provide air cover for this vulnerable transfer of troops. Some of *Canberra*'s crew held up a sign – 'GOOD LUCK 3 PARA'.

HMS *Intrepid* and *Fearless* were known as LPDs, or 'Landing Platform Docks' because they were designed to 'dock down' by pumping sea water into their ballast tanks and then, by opening the stern gates, to flood the area that carried four LCUs (Landing Craft Utility), which could then float out. The sea state that day was only just within the limits for the cross-decking, which was carried out successfully and without injury.

Our packed LCU was guided safely under *Intrepid*'s flight deck and into the dark cavern which was its home. Once there the ramp was lowered and we made our way unsteadily over it and up into the tank deck, where we were met and split into small groups before being guided to various parts of the ship. My sleeping space was on the floor of a bar called 'OIHO', alongside other senior NCO's from Support Company. I had no idea where my men were, and I felt frustrated with a regimental system that seemed obsessed with grouping men into 'messes'; it would have made much more sense at that stage to keep commanders with their own men.

I was told that there were now 1,800 men on board, hundreds more than could comfortably be accommodated, and every available space was occupied. We were instructed not to move around the ship unless it was absolutely necessary. I tried to assemble my men for a rebriefing but it proved impossible – I could find only half of them. I passed one man who had made his bed on a shelf of an empty bookcase, with his equipment and rifle on the shelf below.

Despite the cramped conditions it felt good to be aboard a warship and there was a cheerful atmosphere, helped along in some areas by the crew who as well as giving up their bunks gave away their rum ration. I have nothing but praise for the way that we were looked after by the Royal Navy. *Intrepid*'s crew had little rest and seemed to be almost constantly at 'action stations'. Each time the 'Air Raid Warning Red' alarm was announced the sailors would rush to man their guns and missiles, donning their white 'anti-flash' hoods and gloves as they went.

An unexpected bonus was the fact that, amid all the crowding and confusion, the ship's cooks managed to feed us all regularly and well.

The night before our move from *Canberra* we had been instructed to set our watches back by one hour, but now we were told to advance them four hours to 'Zulu', or Greenwich Mean Time, where they stayed for the duration of the Campaign.

At 10.50 p.m. (Zulu) it was announced that a Sea King had ditched in the sea three-quarters of a mile astern and we were circling to look for survivors. We could only wait helplessly as the crew made repeated rescue attempts, but it was clear from the grim faces of the rescuers when they returned that they had not been completely successful.

The next morning, 20 May, D-Day minus one, I managed to collect together some of the Milan Section and we went to the tank deck to prepare and check our missiles. We would be carrying 18 missiles ashore with us; three for each firing post. In each three-man crew the 'Number One' would carry the firing post, the 'Number Two' two missiles and the 'Number Three' one missile and a radio. When the missiles had been removed from their containers, checked and had slings fitted to them we moved them closer to the landing craft where they would be collected before boarding. The Mortar Platoon were also busy preparing their bombs by removing the protective packaging from them before replacing them in their plastic cylinders. Each man in the Battalion who was not carrying a specialised load would be given two mortar bombs to carry ashore and dump on the beach near the mortar baseplate position.

The Wombat Sections would also go ashore with the rifle companies but, because vehicles would not be available for some time, and the difficulty foreseen in manhandling the heavy guns over the Falklands terrain, they were to act as machine-gun and medium anti-tank teams (with their GPMG and 84mm Carl Gustav weapons). It was planned that the 120mm Wombat guns would be lifted ashore by helicopter as soon as it became practicable, but in fact all six guns were destined to suffer the same fate as the *Green Lanyard* and remain silent aboard *Canberra*.

We were given the sad news that 22 men had perished in the Sea King accident of the night before. They were being cross-decked from HMS *Hermes* and about to land on *Intrepid* when the accident took place. There were only eight survivors from thirty men crammed into the aircraft. I later discovered that one of the SAS dead was a man I knew – he had served in the Para Vigilant Platoon. Rumour had it that an albatross had been found in the cockpit and may have caused the crash; in fact it is believed likely that part of the albatross entered an engine air intake. Another Sea King had crash-landed in Chile but this news arrived with another rumour – that it was no accident and a raid on an Argentine airfield would result, presumably to attack the aircraft capable of launching Exocet missiles.

There were some SAS men on board *Intrepid*, and I recognised one of them as an ex-Para; he told me that he had been on eight different ships so far. I was impressed by the size and variety of their ammunition stock on the tank deck, which included American Stinger anti-aircraft missiles that were allegedly very easy to fire and came with a simple 'Idiot's Guide'. An SAS trooper was later to use a Stinger to shoot down an Argentine aircraft near Darwin.

In the afternoon, at the end of our preparations there remained nothing more to be done, and a few of us went (against orders) on deck, where we could see some of the other ships manoeuvring through the rough seas. The ships were much closer together than they had previously been, and they formed two lines. Low cloud and mist had reduced, but not eliminated, the possibility of air attack. I could see the white mass of *Canberra*, for once well camouflaged in the mist. The carrier HMS *Invincible* was at the rear of the two lines of ships, and I could also see the *Norland* carrying 2 Para.

The remaining hours before the landings were spent sleeping, reading or writing letters. I lifted the lid of a storage box/bench in the OIHO bar and found a Union Jack the size of a bedspread. I have to admit I considered stealing the flag and taking it ashore with me to raise above Port Stanley, but after wrestling with my conscience for a while I eventually decided to leave it, partly because it was so big that it would have been awkward to carry. I settled for the small plastic Union Jack I had been given in the Malet Arms before leaving Tidworth.

A programme of timings was issued, which I have kept (timings in Zulu):

Commanders Office
HMS INTREPID
20 May 1982

INTEM SPECIAL/82
ARGIE-BARGIE OUTLINE PROGRAMME

The following is an outline of the programme within the ship for the period covering the approach to the AOA and the initial assault. It may be necessary for some of these timings to change so KEEP FLEXY.

2300–0030	NAAFI Canteen open.
0130	Hands to ACTION STATIONS
0140	All Embarked Force move to 2 Deck or above. Leave equipment and weapons behind just take lifejacket, survival suit and anti-flash protection.
0210	Ballast Parties close up.
0230	Pass through entrance to Falklands Sound.
0240	Start Ballasting. Embarked Force return to messes to rejoin Kit/Equipment.
0300(Approx)	Ship Anchors. QUARTERS ACTION SNACKS (Ships Co IAW INTEM 37/82)

0315	RM Embarked Forces *not Z Company or 3 Para* are to send one representative from each messdeck to collect snacks from the JRDH.
0330	Embarked Force (Z Coy Gp and 3 Para) proceed to dining hall as piped in order: 1. Z Coy Gp. 2. A Coy 3 Para. 3. B Coy 3 Para. 4. C Coy 3 Para. 5. D Coy + HQ Coy 3 Para.
0600	Assault Stations.
0615	JR Dining Hall to be cleared and tables stacked.
0630	Z Coy Gp and B Coy 3 Para assemble in JR Dining Hall.
0715	Z Coy Gp move to Tank Deck.
0730	B Coy 3 Para move to LCVP Positions. JR Dining Hall prepared for meal.
0745	BREAKFAST for: 1. Ships Company. 2. Embarked force other than Z Coy and 3 Para. Personnel to be released from Action Stations as piped.
0745	Companies of 3 Para start to move to Tank Deck as piped.

Colonel Pike spoke on the pipes and thanked the crew for their hospitality. He also quoted the words of Brigadier Hill, a Brigade Commander of 6 Airborne Division, who addressed his men prior to the Normandy Landings in 1944: 'Do not be daunted if chaos reigns, because it undoubtedly will.' We knew that last-minute diplomacy had failed and that before dawn, if fate allowed, we would be standing on the Falkland Islands.

6. DESTINATION

Finally the excitement of the adventure had seized upon everybody's mind, and the inward choking feeling of dread was overlaid by an outward gaiety, by the exaltation and other-worldness that chloroforms the soldier in the last moments of waiting.

Alan Moorhead, *Gallipoli*

———— •◆• ————

Using my equipment for a pillow I managed some sleep, and woke to realise that *Intrepid* was strangely quiet and still. The ships of the amphibious group had slipped between East and West Falkland and into San Carlos Water, where we were now at anchor.

A frustrating wait followed. We were fed in the dining hall and returned to our positions to wait for our last 'piped' instructions. The landing operation appeared to us, helplessly caged in a ship so close to land, to be conducted with a remarkable lack of urgency, which I assume was not the case.

The first wave consisted of 40 Commando and (a fact that caused us some irritation) 2 Para, who had come late to the party but were now taking 3 Para's place as 'Spearhead'; not only that, but the landing craft from our ship would leave *empty* to go and pick them up from the *Norland*.

Word reached us that there would be a delay due to the slow rate at which 2 Para had been able to board the landing craft; one of them had been badly injured when he was crushed between a landing craft and the side of the ship. The men of 2 Para had not had the benefit of rehearsing this procedure at Ascension Island due to lack of time, and the Captain of the *Norland* had hindered the process by partially lowering his lifeboats.

The LCUs returned to *Intrepid* about an hour later than planned. When I was finally called forward from the galley and took my place

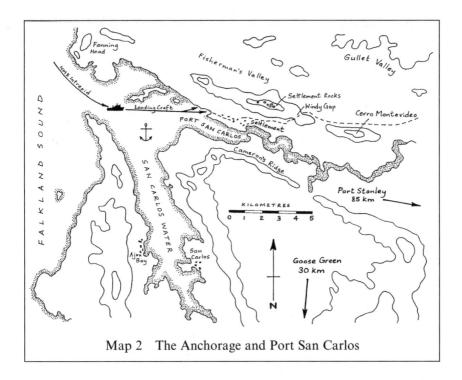

Map 2   The Anchorage and Port San Carlos

in the queue for the landing craft down on the tank deck, I could see that the sky was growing lighter.

My Milan crews collected their missiles and picked up hand grenades before entering the craft. My Section had been allocated white phosphorous grenades to enable us to lay a quick smokescreen if we had to move from exposed positions, but there had been little control of the grenade issue and they had been 'nicked' by the rifle companies ahead of us in the queue. We contented ourselves with HE (High Explosive) grenades, and quickly stuffed them in our pockets and webbing.

We shared a landing craft with C Company and a Scimitar armoured vehicle of the Blues and Royals. It was just after dawn on a clear, sunny day when our LCU backed out of *Intrepid* and we immediately began to scan the surrounding sky for enemy aircraft. Sea King helicopters, which surely could have been used to lift at least some of us ashore, sat idle on deck. Fortunately for us, the only occupants of the San Carlos sky were seagulls and the 4.5 inch shells fired from our ships at the enemy position on Fanning Head to the north of us. We saw the shells explode in the distance and hoped that the Argentines were in the middle of them.

Our progress to the shore seemed painfully slow. We passed the frigate HMS *Argonaut* patrolling the anchorage and, to my amazement, *Canberra*, which was anchored much closer to Port San Carlos than *Intrepid* – where was the sense in that, I wondered? Why was *Intrepid* not anchored closer to the shore, which would have speeded up the whole affair? But the Argentine Air Force missed a golden opportunity to wipe out the whole of the second wave of troops before we reached land, and chaos did not reign after all.

I took photographs with my pocket camera that stayed with me throughout the Campaign. I had also decided to continue my diary, which was wrapped in a plastic bag and shared a pocket of my windproof smock with my syrette of morphine, plus a wound dressing and a bandage.

As our landing craft edged towards Port San Carlos the officers on board, including the commander of the Scimitar, began to discuss the possibility of landing at a different point to the one planned, and decided to change course and land at a spot that favoured the armoured vehicle. It meant that my men would have an extra 800 metres to walk to the designated landing beach and beyond that to the rendezvous with B Company. The decision did, however, mean that we would get on to dry land quicker (I use the word 'dry' because at least it appeared to be so – I actually doubt if the Falklands are ever dry).

At last our steel tub approached land and the bow ramp fell noisily on to the pebble beach before disgorging its load. We splashed through the shallow water and moved away from the C Company men who were headed up the hill towards Settlement Rocks. I felt comfortable now that I could walk on land and have some degree of control over events. I led my line of men towards Port San Carlos and Green One Beach where we should have landed.

After nearly half an hour our small group was approaching Sand Bay when, alerted by the sound of firing, I turned towards the anchorage to see the first of the air attacks. Two white Argentine Skyhawks swooped low over the entrance to the anchorage towards the sunlit bulk of *Canberra*. Tracer and missile trails criss-crossed over the water as the ships fought to stay afloat amid the bombs that exploded in the sea around them. We had taken cover but quickly realised that the aircraft were little threat to us – the Argentine pilots were obviously hunting bigger prey, and although it was tempting to watch, we turned our backs to the battle and continued on our way towards the northern edge of Port San Carlos Settlement.

A Landrover came slowly towards us on the track from the Settlement, and as it passed I raised my hand and smiled at the civilian driver, the first Falkland Islander I had seen. A smile in return would have sufficed to show some gratitude for his liberation, but his grim expression made me wonder if, like many of the features on my map, he had a Spanish name. I learned later that he was carrying the dead body of one of our Gazelle pilots in the back of his vehicle.

Moving through the edge of the Settlement I climbed over a wooden fence surrounding one of the buildings, and as I did so, it collapsed beneath me. 'Shit! – just like Northern Ireland isn't it?' I remarked to a nearby machine-gun team as I picked myself up; but then, as if to prove that it was nothing at all like Northern Ireland, the machine-gun opened fire at two Pucara aircraft as they sped low over Cameron's Ridge to our south to join the attack on the ships. A Blowpipe anti-aircraft detachment behind us also fired at the aircraft, but the missile trailed harmlessly behind its target and exploded in empty sky.

As we continued to trudge upwards, 81mm high-explosive rounds fired by our Mortar Platoon were bursting on The Knob, a small promontory in Port San Carlos: the mortars were 'bedding-in' – firing to embed their mortar baseplates into the ground.

B Company had, quite rightly, not waited for us at the agreed rendezvous, and had pushed on to the Windy Gap objective, where we made contact and I moved forward to site the Milan positions. We then settled into the familiar infantry routine of digging, drawing range cards and more digging. Chris Howard, the Sergeant in the Wombat Section, had sited his machine-gun and Carl Gustav teams and asked if he could join Phil Heyward and me at our position above B Company Headquarters, facing south over Port San Carlos. Chris was an experienced Milan operator, and throughout the Campaign never lost an opportunity to attach himself to my Section, in the hope that a chance to fire a missile would present itself. An extra man with a spade was most welcome, and it was not long before our trench was three feet deep and rapidly filling with water. Deciding not to dig deeper, we gathered large rocks from the surrounding area, and used them to construct walls around the trench for extra protection.

Corporal 'Ginge' McCarthy had a firing post position to our left and was having problems breaking up the rocky ground. In some areas the digging was easier but water was a common problem; all our trenches contained water at least ankle-deep. I constructed a duck-board from a pile of fence posts I had discovered, which helped a little, but we could not keep our feet dry.

Each morning and evening, before dawn and dusk, we observed the ritual of 'stand-to' for an hour – fully dressed and equipped to repel the attacks that never came. Sunsets were usually spectacular. When it was not misty the Falklands air was extremely clear, which made distant objects appear much closer than they actually were. The nights were extremely long – about fourteen hours – which was to our advantage as many of our movements and activities could take place under the relative cover of darkness. Morning stand-to was usually a miserable hour, when Windy Gap really lived up to its name, and the wind usually brought rain. The daylight hours, though, were generally dry, but the ground was constantly wet and boggy.

A winter campaign means that soldiers become burdened with extra protective clothing if they are to remain efficient. I wore basically the same set of clothing from the day I left *Canberra* until I was able to change some items from my follow-up kit 27 days later in Port Stanley. Long johns and long-sleeved vest 'Extreme Cold Weather' were covered by lightweight green trousers and a civilian fibre-pile jacket (I shared a common distaste for Army 'KF' shirts and had left mine behind on the *Canberra*). On top of that I wore an Army pull-over and a camouflaged 'windproof' smock and trousers. In addition I sometimes wore the issued quilted jacket under my smock and occasionally donned quilted trousers. I could cover all of that with a camouflaged waterproof jacket and trousers. I wore two pairs of 'Arctic' socks and I strapped a pair of civilian waxed canvas gaiters over my 'DMS' boots. To keep my spare socks warm and dry I carried them in the front pockets of my lightweight trousers. I wore the issued 'headover' around my neck. My helmet (with red beret tucked inside) was usually replaced by an Arctic issue cap when I considered the threat to my skull to be minimal. I carried leather combat gloves and wore them when they were dry.

Like many men I had supplemented or replaced some of the issued items with my own. The DMS boots we had worn in the Paras during my 12 years of service until then were widely believed to have been unsuitable for the climate of the Falklands, and were blamed for many of the foot injuries suffered. I was happy with my combination of boots and gaiters, and I do not think that any boots available at the time could have prevented wet feet for long.

An item that was available at the time and not issued to 3 Para, although 2 Para and the Marines were issued with it, was a 'sleeping mat' – a closed-cell foam mat that provided insulation from the ground.

The day after the landings Colonel Pike visited us and moved one of the platoons further south down the slope to a new position that gave the Company more depth. The three rifle platoons of B Company had dug in on what was designated the 'reverse slope' of the ridge, which assumed that the north side of the ridge was the forward slope and therefore closer to the enemy. I had chosen my Milan positions to cover an attack from any direction, and the detachments between them could cover all angles of approach, but to do this two of them had to be sited on the lonely northern slope, which was protected only by patrols.

Corporal 'Ollie' Oliver and Private 'Stretch' Dunn commanded the outposts. Stretch and his men had been last in the queue for grenades and had missed out because men in front of them had taken too many, so I gave him one of mine for comfort.

As well as patrols from the rifle companies, the Battalion relied as usual on the patrols of D Company for early warning of enemy movement. The four-man patrols formed a screen well in advance of the main Battalion positions. The patrolling was, in theory, coordinated at Battalion Headquarters. Due to a misunderstanding, patrols from A and C Companies fired on each other, each believing the other to be the enemy. Mortars and machine-guns had joined in, and before the mistake was realised, eight men from A Company had been injured, some seriously. The knowledge that some of the enemy were wearing British uniform captured from the Royal Marines at Moody

Brook may have contributed to the mistake. This 'Blue-on-Blue' incident, and others like it that took place between other units, are unfortunately not uncommon – Northern Ireland has seen many such incidents. Dangerous mistakes will occur, as long as soldiers remain fallible; and fatigue, poor visibility, bad planning and an over-eagerness to engage the enemy are some of the factors that make them more likely.

———— •◆• ————

More bad news came on Sunday, 23 May – HMS *Ardent*, the frigate that had given us such a proud live-firing display on our way south, had been sunk with many casualties.

Rumours, followed by official information, gave details of the deaths of three crewmen from two Gazelle helicopters that had been in support of us on D-Day – due to a lack of co-ordination at Brigade, the aircraft had flown over Port San Carlos before it had been cleared by A Company and both were shot down by a retreating enemy force 43 strong. There was a rumour that one of the crew had been shot in the water as he was swimming towards the shore. If 3 Para had got ashore on time it is likely that the incident would not have occurred, and the enemy force could have been dealt with; instead they made good their escape towards Port Stanley, unseen by the Battalion.

Our trenches on the southern slopes at Windy Gap gave us a grandstand view of the daily air attacks on the ships. The first entry in my diary following D-Day records an air attack at 12.50 p.m. on 23 May – one of the warships was on fire and we were later told that it had been holed but was still serviceable. I had managed to take a photograph as one of the attacking aircraft was shot down by a Rapier missile fired from a position to the west of Port San Carlos. By that time we had a Rapier Detachment on the B Company position at Windy Gap; it sat on the crown of the ridge not far from my trench, having been carried there underneath one of the hard-working Sea Kings. Much to our disgust, the sophisticated anti-aircraft system had developed a problem that had prevented it from firing since its arrival the day before.

Many of the enemy aircraft used the valley of Port San Carlos as a route in or out of the anchorage; flying fast and low, they passed close above our positions and were usually fired at with rifles and machine-guns. Windy Gap became like a large-scale fairground shooting gallery – the fact that there were men inside the targets was almost irrelevant – the challenge was to bring down one of the machines. The correct technique for such an engagement was to fire rapidly ahead of the aircraft and let it fly into the curtain of bullets – simple enough in theory but frustratingly difficult in practice. One man in Headquarters Company down in the Settlement claimed to have shot down a Mirage jet but we were sceptical. After several attempts by most of B Company to bring down a fighter, orders came to hold fire because it was considered a waste of ammunition and, because they flew so low between our positions that there was a risk of hitting our own troops.

Date: *D + 3* [24 May 1982, Monday]
Place: *Windy Gap, Port San Carlos*
Weather: *A beautiful day*
2035 hours [4.35 p.m. local] *Sunset. Still at work on the defensive position – my trench which I share with Chris Howard and Phil Heyward is like a castle – we've used rocks and clay to build walls 2 feet thick – 2 more days should see it fully complete.*

There's a Rapier set up 100 metres behind us on the hill top – it has been unserviceable for the last 2 days and they've just got it going now. This afternoon 2 Mirage attacked the Battalion position and came close overhead – we each emptied a magazine at them then cursed the Rapier detachment for not working. Apparently 4 aircraft were shot down today. 2 PARA have been warned-off for a raid on Goose Green. HMS Antelope has been sunk. Last night we could see huge flashes of light to the South West which could have been the ship exploding. Just going round to check the MILAN positions. Rapier's generator is now noisily at work behind us – hopefully it will do its job tomorrow.

Each evening before stand-to as B Company sent patrols out for the night I would visit the Milan crews and pass on any information I had gained from Major Argue's daily O Group.

Tony Dunn, B Company's Colour Sergeant, had managed to deliver our bergens to the position by the second day ashore, and later some scrounged corrugated metal sheets arrived to be used for support for overhead protection. Our trench had two sleeping bays covered by rocks supported by fence posts. I had decorated the roof of one of the sleeping bays with rows of sheep's skulls as totems, and the trench had taken on the appearance of an entrance to a mystical underworld.

Date: *D + 4* [25 May 1982]
Place: *Windy Gap*
Weather: *Another fair day – windy!*
A fairly uneventful day apart from a Mirage which flew past – the Rapier behind us fired but missed.

Shaved today. Feet wet – trench foot is going to be a problem. 2 PARA not attacking Goose Green now because 600 enemy there. One of the MILAN detachments with C Company fired a missile at a Mirage yesterday with no chance of hitting.

Finished the second shelter bay today – starting on another fire trench tomorrow.

The Commanding Officer visited B Company at Windy Gap again on Wednesday 26 May, and from him we learned that we would be staying put to await the arrival of 5 Infantry Brigade, which was depressing news. We were certain that the two Parachute Battalions and three Commandos, plus the SAS, SBS and supporting arms, constituted a strong enough force to complete the job. The fact that 5 Brigade was made up of Guards and Gurkhas did not inspire optimism either. Despite the rivalry between the Maroon and Green 'Machines', there was an underlying mutual respect, and I preferred to fight alongside the Marines than the Guards or the Gurkhas. The Guards, I believed, spent too much time on 'spit and polish' and marching around London rather than training for war; in fact the Guardsmen sent to join us were fresh from a period of 'public duties'. Even the Gurkhas, in my opinion, were vastly over-rated, and I would have preferred to see a brigade with three battalions from any other infantry regiment.

Scoop McGachen had arrived with Colonel Pike and came into our trench to share a brew of tea. He was unhappy with his job as the Company Quartermaster Sergeant of HQ Company because it was an administrative post and kept him out of the front line.

Date: *D* + *5* [26 May 1982]
Place: *Windy Gap*
Weather: *Sunny*
1725 hours [1.25 p.m. local]*: Mirage aircraft just bombed positions to the South of here – 2 PARA?*

Looks like we may be here for some time. Heard that HMS Coventry *is sunk and that* Atlantic Conveyor *has been hit by 2 Exocets and is being towed here.*

An over-snow vehicle has just brought up stores.

Apparently Canberra *has gone back to Ascension to pick up 5 Brigade from the* QE2 *which can't be risked in the war zone.*

Everyone here just wants to get to Stanley and finish it off.

The over-snow vehicle referred to was a **BV 202**; a tracked, articulated tractor and trailer used for carrying troops and equipment, sometimes called a Bandwagon. They were in use at the time with the Marines and Army units assigned to the Arctic Warfare role.

The following day there was a dramatic change to the strategy, and the Battalion was given orders to advance and capture Teal Inlet, a Settlement on the way to Port Stanley. 45 Commando were to move to Douglas Settlement and 40 Commando were to take over the defence of the anchorage. 2 Para tabbed south from Sussex Mountain for their 'raid' on Goose Green. The Brigade Commander, Brigadier Thompson, had originally wanted 3 Para to follow 45 Commando to Douglas before turning east towards Teal, but Colonel Pike had learned that there was a better, more direct route, which the Brigadier agreed to. Finally, we were leaving the beachhead, and 3 Para would be leading the way to Stanley – that was more like it!

7. ADVANCE

Beware of over exposure to the sun when out of the wind.
Advice from an information sheet issued to troops aboard the
Canberra about dangers likely to be faced on the Falklands

———— •◆• ————

Leaving behind their bergens, and preceded as usual by the patrols of
Patrol Company, the three rifle companies began their tab on the
afternoon of Thursday 27 May. They moved in light order to speed
their march – a bold decision that relied on helicopters or other
transport to follow at a later stage with their bergens, containing their
sleeping bags, rations and warm clothing necessary to remain effective in that climate. The Mortar Platoon had acquired two tractors
and trailers from the Settlement, and followed the rifle companies,
ready to give support if necessary.

I was instructed to remain behind with my Milan Section. The
defence of the useless Rapier detachment at Windy Gap was now in
my hands, and I repositioned Corporal Whittle's crew. Chris Howard
and his men, having been told that their Wombat guns and vehicles
would not be brought ashore, departed on foot with B Company.

45 Commando plodded slowly past our positions just before dark,
burdened with their heavy equipment, and there was a marked contrast between the marching speeds of 3 Para and 45 Commando.
Although 45 Commando marched (or 'yomped', as they called it)
much more slowly than 3 Para, they would at least be able to remain
effective longer if re-supply was impossible; on the other hand they
would be quickly exhausted under their heavy loads. They certainly
appeared better equipped than us, with their issued gaiters and
sleeping mats; the latter making me envious when I later spread my
sleeping bag on the cold, damp floor of my trench.

Our seventh and final night at Windy Gap was again uneventful, and the following day I was given orders by radio to move down the hill into Port San Carlos Settlement. An OP (Observation Post) team from 40 Commando took up a position in the rocks above the saddle before we trudged off, carrying all our Milan equipment and bergens. Private Pat Harley had strapped a missile to each side of his bergen and appeared to be carrying some kind of jet-powered flying machine; it must have weighed about a hundred and fifty pounds, and required two men to help him put it on his back.

As we descended we could see the wreckage of one of the ill-fated Gazelle helicopters down near the water to the east of the Settlement, and we passed the remains of one of the parachute-retarded bombs dropped during one of the Argentine air attacks.

Port San Carlos Settlement consisted of about twenty wooden houses and sheep shearing huts. We passed through to the south side of the buildings and occupied some of A Company's abandoned trenches to the east of the airstrip. There was some abandoned enemy equipment in the area and the Quartermaster had acquired an Argentinian officer's ceremonial sword. In my new trench (of poor quality compared to the one I had vacated at Windy Gap) I found a groundsheet which had belonged to an Argentine soldier before being used by one of our A Company men; it carried a label with the name 'AIME NORBERTO' on it – perhaps he was by now at the end of his long walk to Port Stanley. It felt odd to think that he and I might soon try to kill each other.

The Commanding Officer and his Tactical Headquarters had moved with the rifle platoons, and the small force remaining behind at The Settlement was commanded by his second-in-command, who, in the style of the Grand Old Duke of York, told me that he needed my men on Settlement Rocks, C Company's old position. There had been no change to the situation since the order to leave our positions, and it angered me to have to send Corporal Mathews and his two Milan crews back up the hill to their old trenches for the night; incidents such as this (fortunately not common), tended to lead to a lack of confidence in the ability of our commanders to make logical and wise decisions.

While most of 3 Para struggled through bogs towards Teal Inlet and my Milan Section trudged up and down hills at Port San Carlos for no clear reason, 2 Para were in action at Goose Green. Some fragments of information began to filter back to us that evening, including the news that 2 Para's Commanding Officer, Colonel 'H' Jones, had been killed.

That night, 28 May, a stew was cooked centrally for those of us left behind at Port San Carlos, but the remainder of the Battalion were tired, cold and hungry as they closed on Teal Inlet, seizing the Settlement unopposed at 10.45 p.m.

After our meal at Port San Carlos, Colour Sergeant Graham Russell of Support Company showed me to a garden shed where an Islander, introduced to me as Ron, was tuning an old wireless set to the BBC frequency. The scene in the dimly lit shed as the radio whistled and crackled to life conjured up a picture of paratroopers of forty years before receiving help from an underground resistance unit. As we expected, however, the announcer told us nothing that we did not already know, but it was good to hear news of 2 Para's exploits broadcast around the world.

On the following morning Corporal Mathews and his men were called back down from Settlement Rocks and my Milan Section prepared to fly by helicopter to join the Battalion at Teal Inlet.

There were clear skies as the Sea King lifted off and flew fast and low over the desolate land between Port San Carlos and Teal Inlet. The helicopter crewman in the open door had his machine-gun ready but the only sign of life was a flock of sheep that scattered as we passed. We landed at the edge of a small collection of wooden buildings and a few stunted trees (the first and only ones I saw on the Island) as the rifle companies were deploying into new defensive positions.

As bright sunshine gave way to showers of sleet, I sited two Milan crews with each of the three rifle companies, and once again we began to dig. Phil the sniper and I dug our trench in soft earth inside a wire mesh compound of a chicken run, not far from Support Company Headquarters near the Settlement Manager's house. The absence of the former occupants of the chicken hut was a disappointment.

More helicopters arrived carrying under-slung loads, and grateful men collected their bergens from the nets, which also contained mortar bombs and rations. The decision to travel light and rely on helicopters for heavy lift appeared to be paying off.

A young 2nd Lieutenant, commander of the Machine-Gun

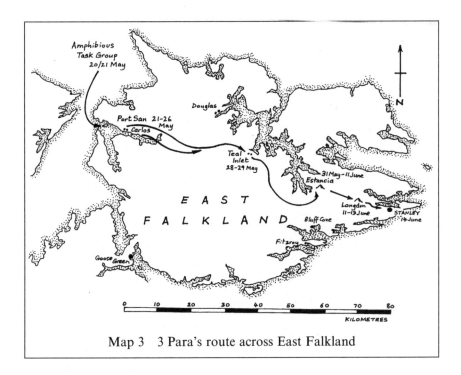

Map 3   3 Para's route across East Falkland

Platoon, asked if he could join us in our hole, and helped with the digging. We were soon at a sufficient size and depth for a three-man fire trench and then we added a shelter bay that the three of us could just squeeze into after we had covered it with wood and earth. I ripped some linoleum from the floor of the hut and used it to carpet the bottom of the trench, and when I had fixed my Union Jack to the fence we were ready for stand-to in our hole, facing north over an empty field and the calm waters of the Inlet.

That night, rather than spend another night underground, Phil and I chose to sleep in the chicken hut. We were woken for a two-hour duty, or 'stag', at the Support Company HQ position but apart from that slept soundly until woken for the dawn stand-to. The unaccustomed heat inside the hut had brought hundreds of bluebottle flies to life, and it was a relief to escape the buzzing and the smell and get out into the cold air. A thin carpet of snow covered the field in front of our trench as we waited for daylight and had time to contemplate what the day might bring. Two years after my stay in the chicken hut I

99

met a man in Edmonton, Canada, who remembered collecting eggs from the same hut as a boy.

There was some welcome sunshine later in the day and the snow melted. A giant Chinook helicopter loaded with ammunition and stores landed in the field next to the Settlement Manager's house. The Chinook was the only survivor of four such aircraft that had been transported by the doomed *Atlantic Conveyor*. It took away a prisoner who had surrendered to the Battalion the previous day. Not relishing the prospect of a long walk to Stanley, the Argentine soldier had threatened one of the Teal residents with a pistol and demanded the keys to a vehicle. The man obligingly handed over the keys, neglecting to tell the enemy soldier that the vehicle had been disabled. Unable to start the engine, he eventually surrendered to A Company after spending some time under the protection of the Settlement Manager, who had had to be persuaded that the man would not be executed. The prisoner was the first enemy soldier I had seen, and I recorded the event with a photograph before he was taken aboard the Chinook.

Stories of 2 Para at Goose Green circulated. Someone had spoken to someone else who had met another man who had witnessed 2 Para's attack in a liaison role, and it was described as, 'Like Arnhem' – rather an exaggerated comparison obviously, but we knew what he meant; this was *war* – not 'peacekeeping' in Northern Ireland – this was the real thing, war in all its exhilarating, terrifying, spectacular bloody glory – something that until then we had only read about in books or seen in films. The story also circulated that the Argentines at Goose Green had killed two 2 Para men who had gone forward under a flag of truce to take the surrender of an enemy unit – this caused widespread anger and we became determined not to fall into the same trap.

———— •◆• ————

Our stay at Teal Inlet was a short one and orders were soon issued to continue the advance eastwards. I decided to leave my tiny Union Jack on the fence, as once again bergens were centralised to reduce our loads in preparation for the next leg of the advance, which would begin in daylight and take us to Estancia House, a farm that stood 25

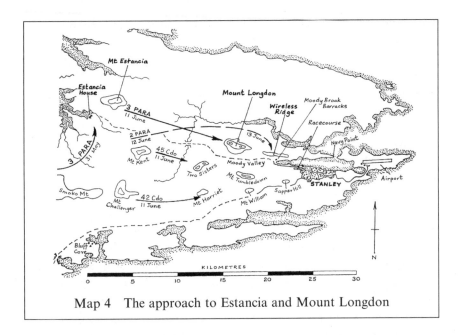

Map 4   The approach to Estancia and Mount Longdon

kilometres away from Teal as the crow flew, but our route would take us in a much longer loop to the south around the many inlets. 45 Commando, who had occupied Douglas Settlement, were to 'yomp' from there to Teal and then follow 3 Para.

A tractor that towed a sledge was provided for the Milan firing posts and missiles. The tractor was driven by a young Islander called Dave, who handled the six-wheeled vehicle expertly. We soon realised, as the sledge ground its way over the rocks and 'diddle-dee' (as the long grass was called by the locals), that the tractor had more than enough power to take on some passengers, and the Milan men jumped aboard.

We were soon passed by a tractor that was towing a trailer and heading back toward the Settlement. A smiling Graham Russell sat in the trailer keeping careful aim at two more prisoners who had surrendered as the Battalion advanced; we assumed that the men, and the other already taken prisoner, were stragglers from the group that had vacated Port San Carlos (and shot down the Gazelles) during the landings nine days earlier.

Apart from 'our' tractor and sledge, the Mortar Platoon occupied

101

the remainder of the borrowed transport and the rest of the Battalion tabbed in open formation ahead of us, led by Patrol Company. We were accompanied by Scimitar and Scorpion light reconnaissance tanks of the Blues and Royals, as well as their recovery vehicle that was being used to carry a Royal Artillery Blowpipe detachment. By this stage I had seen two Blowpipe missiles miss the aircraft they were aimed at, and I had no confidence that they would be able to protect us if we were attacked from the air.

It was still daylight when we paused at a bridge over a ravine near Lower Malo House. Entertainment was provided by a 3 Para soldier on the far side of the ravine who, presumably in the act of shielding his stove from the wind, managed to set fire to his clothing. Laughter and cheering echoed around the ravine until it was angrily silenced.

The tab continued as darkness fell. It was a particularly dark night, despite the clear sky, and at one point my Section became separated from the column of men in front of us, who could not be seen. I climbed on to one of the cavalry vehicles nearby and asked the commander to search the ground ahead with his image-intensifier gun sight; he was then able to indicate the correct direction to take. Although a track of sorts connected Teal Inlet and Estancia House, it often seemed to diverge and split into several tracks that took different routes.

After two or three hours of the night move we received orders to halt and 'lie-up' until daylight. The night was freezing cold and we were without our sleeping bags. We wrapped ourselves in our waterproof 'ponchos' and tried in vain to sleep. Wearing all my clothing but chilled to the bone, the nearest I could come to sleep was to achieve a kind of semi-dream state, with the wind and the stamping of feet on the frozen earth a constant background noise.

The longed-for daylight brought with it at least an illusion of warmth, and a chance to inspect our numb and shrivelled feet. I massaged my bare feet until it was time to move on again, and advised my men to do the same. Having suffered the agonies of trench foot before, I was conscious that our feet were approaching that same condition.

The advance was resumed in clear daylight, a challenge to the enemy that we assumed must be watching us from the range of hills to our south. The engineers of 9 Para Squadron attached to the

Battalion were carrying bergens full of their specialist gear and were grateful to be invited to put them on our sledge. Most of my men who had ridden on the sledge now chose to walk in an attempt to bring some feeling back to their feet.

As several hundred men marched ahead of me, appearing like so many soldier ants as the various company and platoon columns stretched into the distance across the open, undulating ground, it felt good to be moving towards the enemy, and to be doing so in broad daylight as if heedless of the threat.

During our advance one of the armoured vehicles became stuck in a ditch, an unusual occurrence for those light tanks that could negotiate most types of terrain. Another of its family came to the rescue and by using a connecting rope with elastic properties and applying tension at speed, pulled the stricken vehicle forward on to firmer ground.

The lines of men and vehicles continued to edge closer to Estancia House throughout the day, until we halted in a creek to wait for darkness to cover our final approach. The Mortars were made ready for action to give covering fire if needed and at last light patrols were sent forward to check the farm, later reporting the area free of enemy troops. A Company then moved past the farm up into the hills beyond. It was Monday, 31 May – four days after we had set out from Port San Carlos – and from the hills above Estancia House the lights of Port Stanley could be seen over twenty kilometres to the east.

Mount Kent, four kilometres to the south-east of Estancia House, had been occupied by D Squadron 22 SAS for several nights, reinforced later by part of 42 Commando and some artillery guns that were flown forward by helicopters.

I spent the remainder of the night at the farm with the rest of the Milan Section and Support Company Headquarters. Dave, our driver, sought shelter at the farmhouse. I found a place to lie down at the side of a sheep-shearing shed and optimistically hoped to find sleep there. The shed was occupied by men of Patrol Company, who temporarily enjoyed its relative warmth and shelter before resuming their patrol tasks. Our sleeping bags were still back at Teal Inlet and so another freezing, shivering, skeleton-rattling night ensued. Denzil Connick, the Anti-tank Platoon signaller, had settled into a spot close to me and we ended up huddled together in a makeshift shelter and waited for daylight.

In the morning I found Dave and he drove us across the wet sands of the inlet and up on to Estancia Mountain and Mount Vernet where I deployed the Milan crews with the rifle companies. The men of A Company were at that stage in amongst the rocks on the southern slopes of Mount Estancia. Major Collet, their commander, explained to me that they were not yet properly deployed; nevertheless I sited two firing posts to cover the possible approaches of enemy armour. It seemed much more likely now that we were on the enemy's doorstep that we would have to defend against at least a probing attack, if not a full-scale assault on our relatively small and isolated positions.

As the firing posts were set up a Gazelle helicopter hovered over the position and dropped an under-slung load of a few bergens.

Back at Estancia House I thanked Dave and said goodbye before he began the long journey home to Teal Inlet Settlement. Like all the Islanders I met, Dave was a cheerful and hardy individual. He told us that it was not unusual for him to get drunk in Stanley before riding a motorbike all the way to Teal in time for the next day's work.

Our much-missed bergens were once more ferried forward by Sea Kings and stacked in company rows according to their coloured patches. I carried a list of numbers that enabled me to pick out the rucksacks belonging to my men. An assortment of vehicles was now parked at the farm and a group of Islanders waited like taxi drivers for the next fare. A smiling tractor-driver was happy to help me load my men's bergens into his trailer and drive up to the forward positions to deliver them. When I had completed my delivery round I sent the tractor back down to the farm and found myself a protected nook in the rocky slope of Estancia Mountain below the Commanding Officer's Tactical Headquarters, which consisted of Colonel Pike, the RSM and a couple of signallers in a large hole with radio antennae protruding from it. Phil and I erected a poncho as rain began to fall.

The exposed hilltop was not a comfortable place to spend two hours on 'stag' in the middle of the night after over sixty hours without sleep, but as the wind-driven rain lashed my face I could see the lights of Port Stanley and I was cheered by the fact that the men defending the town would be cursing the same weather.

The next day was misty and wet as I received orders for the Milan Section to regroup back at Estancia House in preparation for a

Battalion attack. The move was accomplished by mid-afternoon, again with the assistance of local transport.

We occupied a large corrugated metal barn of incomplete construction but which gave shelter from the rain if not from the wind. I shaved for the second time since D-Day and wrote in my neglected diary:

> *Tomorrow night our objective is Mount Longdon – 42 Commando are to take Two Sisters tonight . . . The Battalion is very weary and many have bad feet. There is a strong rumour that we will be in Stanley by the weekend.*

It was then Wednesday.

The following morning, 3 June, Major Dennison returned from the Commanding Officer's O Group and briefed us on the plan of attack. After telling us that he thought the CO had gone mad (not exactly a morale-boosting statement) he informed us that the Two Sisters feature had not been attacked during the night by 42 Commando as planned; nevertheless, 3 Para were to attack Mount Longdon that night after a Battalion 'Advance to Contact'. For my part, I was happy to hear any orders that contained the words 'advance' and 'contact'. The plan had a heroic simplicity that suited my mood.

An Advance to Contact by the whole Battalion was a manoeuvre that we had practised occasionally in peacetime (although always in daylight), most recently in Canada the year before when we had used live ammunition. It required the three rifle companies to advance in battle formation, usually with one company forward and two to the rear. The leading company normally adopted a similar formation with two platoons side-by-side to the rear and the third platoon in front – that platoon having one of its three sections of eight men forward, commanded by a corporal. The whole wedge-shaped mass would be supported by advancing SF machine-guns and anti-tank weapons (Milan in this case), and by the Battalion's six mortars. Enemy troops encountered during the advance would be dealt with as appropriate with quick orders and practised 'battle drills' (as opposed to a pre-planned 'Deliberate Attack').

The Blues and Royals Troop would be on hand in this advance to give support with their light tanks. Presumably in this case also we would have some artillery support and perhaps naval gunfire and Harriers in the FGA role might be on call, although there was no mention of it.

Extra Milan missiles had been brought up to Estancia House by the over-worked helicopters, and I acquired another tractor with a sledge to carry them forward to the area north of Mount Kent where the rifle companies were deploying to begin their advance. The SF machine-gun teams and my Milan crews, along with the Anti-tank Platoon Headquarters, left the farm on foot and followed a difficult route up and across the rocky hillside where I found our waiting tractor and sledge.

After a short wait we began the advance towards Mount Longdon, ten kilometres away but shrouded in mist on an otherwise clear and sunny afternoon. There was a real 'Death or Glory – into the Valley of Death' feel to the advance, as we were certain to attract artillery fire well before we finally approached the objective in darkness.

We had not gone far before we were ordered to 'go firm', and then to turn back – the attack was aborted. Denzil Connick, who had been tabbing ahead of me, had heard the order on his radio, and turned and laughed before shouting, 'Run away!' as three 155mm artillery shells landed near us, causing no casualties.

Rumour quickly spread that Brigadier Thompson had flown up in a helicopter to personally order Colonel Pike to abort the attack. Still – 'Better to have to restrain the noble stallion, than to prod the reluctant mule', as I believe an Israeli General once said.

The rifle companies were to return to their trenches and the Milan crews to Estancia House. The armoured vehicles of the Blues and Royals that had been accompanying the advance were also sent to the farm, and I stopped them to ask for a lift. My men climbed aboard and clung to the vehicles which sped away, leaving Corporal 'Ollie' Oliver and myself to re-adjust the Milan load on its sledge before hitching a lift behind the tractor driver. It grew dark as we approached the bottom of the hill and the tractor lurched over a boulder, throwing me to the ground where I was almost crushed beneath the advancing sledge. As I remounted the tractor I thought about how close I had come to an inglorious death.

When I finally arrived back at what had now become Battalion Headquarters I returned to my floor space of the previous night with mixed feelings about the aborted attack, eventually deciding that it was probably a good thing that it did not go ahead. I have often wondered since if we could have pulled it off – Mount Longdon was reinforced before our eventual attack. It would either have been hailed a stunning and glorious victory or it would have been a costly and unnecessary disaster.

8. DELAY

. . . what have we acquired? What, but a bleak and gloomy solitude, an island thrown aside from human use, stormy in winter, and barren in summer; an island which not the southern savages have dignified with habitation; where a garrison must be kept in a state that contemplates with envy the exiles of Siberia . . .

Samuel Johnson, 'Thoughts on the late Transaction respecting Falkland's Islands', 1771

———— •◆• ————

After stand-to on the morning of 4 June, we moved out of the barn and erected shelters along the fences and gorse hedgerows to the east of the farmhouse. At this time the length of our stay at Estancia was uncertain, and it was possible, we hoped, that the offensive would be quickly resumed; but rumours to the contrary soon circulated.

Estancia House was the home of Tony and Ailsa Heathman, who lived there with their baby daughter. Ailsa's parents had been arrested by the Argentines and taken to Fox Bay. The property consisted of the house itself plus four or five outbuildings that were all put to good use by various elements of 3 Para. Major Dennison and his Support Company Headquarters occupied a shed by the mouth of a stream that ran into the waters of the Inlet. I used a wire fence next to a row of gorse bushes to support one side of my poncho and then secured the other side to the ground. This provided me with reasonable shelter but I was fed up with lying on the bare, damp earth so I went in search of suitable material for a bed. Finding some wooden fence poles I laid them in my shelter to form a solid wooden floor that gave me some insulation from the ground. My new home gave good protection from the elements but not, of course, from attack, although it was away from the buildings that were likely to

108

attract any fire from either ground or air. I did not want to start digging another trench while we were likely to have to move.

I took advantage of the presence of armoured vehicles at Estancia to heat up my feet; I climbed on to a Scorpion light tank and sat on the turret next to its 76mm gun with my feet on the hot engine covers, and before long my feet were burning and my leather boots were thoroughly dry for the first time in two weeks. I then took some grease from a can carried by the vehicle crew and smeared it all over my boots and gaiters, afterwards feeling very pleased with myself. The cavalrymen invariably kept warm in their heated vehicles and had the ability to boil water in electric 'boiling vessels'. They had a rather quaint and appropriate nickname for us footsloggers, calling us, 'Puddle-Jumpers'. Not long after my warming on the Scorpion, the Blues and Royals Troop left us to join 5 Infantry Brigade who were landing on the coast to the south.

Chris Howard came down the hill in the afternoon and once again attached himself to the Milan Section, having convinced Major Argue, the B Company Commander, that he would be better employed with Support Company. Chris immediately expressed his intention to start a fire to dry his clothing and went off to scavenge the area, returning not long after with a wooden wheelbarrow containing peat and an empty oil drum which he then proceeded to attack with a pick. We filled the perforated drum with peat and before long we were warming ourselves around a glowing fire.

Whenever the weather allowed helicopters arrived with more rations and ammunition for the Battalion, but their main task at that stage was to carry forward more 105mm Light Guns and shells to a Battery position behind our forward companies. Our Mortar Platoon had moved forward from their first position near the farm and was now close enough to engage the enemy forward positions on Two Sisters, which they frequently did with some success. A constant problem for the 'Mortars' was the tendency of their baseplates to gradually disappear into the soft Falklands earth under the pressure of successive firings. When the baseplates went too far below ground level they would have to be dug out and moved to another spot. The abandoned mortar position near the farm revealed some useful materials that could be re-used in the construction of our defences, including several sheets of 'wriggly tin', which were dragged over to our brazier where Chris, Ollie, Phil and myself planned to dig a trench.

My diary entry for 4 June reads,

Rumour as usual is rife – the latest is that we will not be attacking Stanley
. . . There are now signs that the war could drag on much longer.

Shortly after stand-down that night a stick of bombs was dropped from a high-flying Argentine aircraft, assessed to be a Canberra (British made). Although the bombs landed at least five hundred metres from my shelter I felt the blast, and the ground shook from the explosions. The intended target was either Estancia House or a group of Sea Kings that were stationed for the night in a re-entrant at the foot of Mount Estancia, but daylight revealed no damage – the only effect was to spur our efforts at excavation.

Three of my men were confirmed as having trench foot, and stayed with the growing number of other sufferers in the barn. Two of the three were later diagnosed as frostbite cases.

More Milan missiles arrived, giving us a total of 37 at Estancia. Our heavy test equipment came up with the missiles, which enabled us to carry out electrical tests on the firing posts, revealing a fault with one of the six that could only be dealt with by a skilled technician in a workshop. The three sick men likewise reduced the Milan crew numbers to five, and I reorganised the Section accordingly.

Trench foot, or immersion foot, is a debilitating condition in its advanced stage and recovery is a slow process. Most of the Battalion were probably sufferers to some extent but able to carry on. Added to the men wounded by 'friendly fire', I reckon the Battalion had lost nearly forty of its fighting strength – none of it caused by enemy fire. The longer the delay in getting to grips with the enemy, the weaker we would become; but I do not believe that the weakening was proportionate to the time spent in the harsh environment – most of us, having got through the first two weeks in reasonable condition, had adapted to the conditions and developed ways of minimising the effects of the cold and wet on our bodies. There was a mental strain, of course, but most of the effects of that would only become evident later, when the danger became severe.

Our adversaries on the ground were obviously suffering the effects of climate also, and had been for over seven weeks. Added to that they had been bombed and shelled from the air and the sea since 1 May, and recently subject to harassing fire from our mortars and artillery. On the other hand they had had ample time in their static positions to construct shelter from the weather and protection from our weapons.

Our shelter at Estancia was beginning to take shape. We had decided to dig a large hole that would provide comfort as well as protection. Comfort was a high priority at that stage, as it usually is with infantry soldiers – which reminds me of the riflemen who tore down the defensive gates of a farmhouse before the Battle of Waterloo to use as firewood. Our primary enemy at the time, unless we were patrolling into no man's land, was not the Argentines – it was the weather, and the maintenance of our defences against it became an obsession. We found a spade in the farmyard that was larger than the ones we carried, and it speeded our digging – until the handle broke. The deeper our hole became the more surprised we were when it did not start to fill with water – it was the only trench I knew of that stayed dry, and it was also warm – when it was large enough we put the glowing oil drum inside it. The peat in the brazier was never allowed to burn out; the farm had a small hill of the stuff already cut for the winter and we made frequent trips to it with the wheelbarrow. Of course the rifle companies in their forward positions were not so fortunate; their battle for comfort on the bare, waterlogged slopes of Mount Estancia and Mount Vernet was often a losing one. The barn at Estancia began to be used as a rest area and the rifle companies began to take turns to enjoy its relative comfort.

Mount Longdon remained our elusive objective. A plan for a 'Deliberate Attack' was formulated that included Milan and SF machine-guns in a fire support role. Major Dennison reorganised the Company into fire teams with a mixture of Milan and machine-guns in each. I was one of the three fire-team commanders and as such I took part in a reconnaissance patrol to look for positions to the west and north-west of Longdon from where we could put fire on to the objective when the time came for the planned attack. The Anti-tank Platoon Commander, Captain Mason, was one of the fire-team commanders and was in charge of the recce patrol that comprised his radio operator Denzil Connick and the other fire-team commanders, 'Shakespeare' Knights and myself. Chris Howard came along and we were also joined by one of the many Islanders that had congregated at Estancia, who was keen to act as a guide; his name was Vernon and he had managed to acquire a rifle, presumably from one of the men in the barn. In the late afternoon a Bandwagon carried us towards the forward positions, stopping to wait for a mortar fire controller who was to join the patrol to look for a baseplate position for the mortars. While we waited for the MFC to join us and for darkness to fall, Chris and I walked down to an abandoned enemy position below Mount Kent, attracted by the wreckage of two enemy helicopters: a Puma and a Chinook. The casing of a nearby cluster bomb indicated that the destruction of the helicopters was the work of our Harrier pilots. Inside the remains of the Chinook I found a charred page from its maintenance manual, printed in English (the Chinook was made in the USA, the Puma in France), and kept it as a souvenir. There were also some bunkers – one that was particularly large and well constructed with a solid roof appeared to have been the enemy's kitchen and contained a large stainless steel cooking-pot and several sacks of rice. There were also long belts of 7.62mm machine-gun ammunition. We took the cooking-pot, the rice and as many belts of ammunition as we could carry (it was same calibre as our ammunition and could be used in our guns) and returned to the Bandwagon with it.

As darkness fell we left the driver with his vehicle to await our return and began to patrol towards Mount Longdon. Our objective, rising above the surrounding peat bogs, lay ten kilometres away at the eastern side of no man's land, which was a vast, empty expanse of undulating, soggy earth and rock outcrops. To the south of us, on our right, ran the track connecting Estancia House with Port Stanley. The track was the designated boundary between 3 Para and the Commandos, so we kept well clear of it to avoid a possible firefight with friendly patrols.

About an hour and a half after leaving our vehicle we approached a stream that crossed our route as it flowed northward to feed the Murrel River. The track to Port Stanley crossed the stream at the Murrel Bridge, away to the right of the spot we had chosen to cross. We observed the area for some time, looking for signs of enemy patrols, observation posts or possible ambush positions before moving down to wade through the icy water of the knee-deep stream. The MFC selected his baseplate position on the western slope of a low hill that stretched eastward towards Mount Longdon, and we continued in that direction, a little more carefully now. In England, a hill the size of Longdon would never qualify as a 'Mount', but as the dark silhouette of the hill loomed ominously before us it seemed to deserve the title.

Across the valley to our right were the enemy occupied hills of Two Sisters, and we were also aware that we were now well within range of the 105mm artillery in Stanley, as well as any machine-guns and support weapons that may have been on Mount Longdon itself.

An 'Emergency RV', a spot where we would all meet after we had completed our tasks, or in case of trouble, was agreed before we split up to look for likely positions for our fire teams for the intended attack. The best positions I could find were some small depressions that could offer very limited protection from enemy fire. I memorised the location and made a small sketch in my notebook of the outline of Mount Longdon as it appeared from that position, before returning to the RV where I met up with Chris Howard.

There was no sign of life on the hill above us. Chris had the only night sight in our patrol, an image-intensifier known as an IWS (Individual Weapon Sight), which he used to scan the area, and while looking across the valley towards Two Sisters, Chris became excited and told me that he could see some enemy trucks. I aimed my binoculars in the same direction but could not see the trucks, so I exchanged rifles with Chris to see for myself, hardly believing that the Argentines could put trucks in such a vulnerable forward position – closer to our front line than we then were. The circular green image presented by the night sight revealed the outline of several vehicles, and although we could not see any men an occasional dim light showed as the canvas flaps covering their interiors were parted. The trucks were widely spread across the valley several hundred metres from us, and we counted seven of them before debating the wisdom of attacking them, possibly by throwing grenades inside them. When the others returned to the RV it was agreed that the best thing to do was to move to a suitable position and get the MFC and to call in mortar or artillery fire on to the trucks.

We moved back along the low hill and found cover in some rocks where Denzil's radio was used to request an artillery 'Fire Mission'. The gunners obviously agreed that the target was important enough for their limited stock of shells, and it was not long before the first adjusting round whistled over and crashed into the valley below us. Corrections were given by the MFC, 'Right two hundred, drop two hundred' and another shell exploded near the target; the enemy in the trucks must have started to get concerned by now. After another correction a third shell exploded on target and 'Fire for Effect' was ordered. A salvo of 105mm high-explosive shells fell among the trucks, followed by another correction, 'Drop one hundred – repeat', and again the valley was lit by six flashes as the shells landed – one of them at least fell alongside an enemy vehicle. Chris regarded the whole fire mission as a birthday present for him, because the shells fell just after midnight (Zulu) on 5 June, and his birthday was 6 June.

Vernon was sat near me in the rocks and I could see that he was smiling as I chewed my way through a packet of 'Biscuits, Fruit, AB' from my rations that I had carried in my pocket (no one knew what AB stood for, but we named them 'Airborne').

The gunners asked what effect their fire had had on the target, and Captain Mason told Denzil to say, 'Target neutralised' – in this case a rather vague and misleading term – it was impossible to say what damage had been caused; there were no burning trucks or secondary explosions or screams of pain. At this stage it was decided not to push our luck and to head for home, back through the stream towards our front lines. As we left Mount Longdon and the stream behind us we heard the distinctive sound of a Huey helicopter in the valley and hoped that it had been called in to evacuate casualties.

My nerves had long since ceased to transmit messages from my feet as we splashed quickly and noisily through the bogs towards our waiting vehicle, which returned us to Estancia House at 11 p.m. It had been a successful patrol – we had got to know the detail of the terrain and we had found the best possible positions for our weapons, given the limitations of the area that had been assigned to us. We had also managed to cause some fire to be directed at the enemy, hopefully to some effect.

The following day we stoked the peat fire and were drying our clothing around it when mail arrived – the second bag since the landings – there had been another one at Windy Gap. The arrival of mail was always a great boost to morale; the very fact that resources could be spared to deliver it seemed to indicate that things were not going quite so badly as we had imagined. Despite the sunken ships and the shortage of helicopters, here was a response to my letter to the Prime Minister and a parcel containing a book I had requested from a friend – a copy of the collected poems of Dylan Thomas.

Reading poetry would not have appeared in the average para-trooper's list of favourite pastimes, but I found Ginge McCarthy, one of the Milan detachment commanders, in his hole at Estancia reading an anthology of British poetry sent to him by his wife. He carried the poems with him to his death six days later.

The letter from the Prime Minister's Private Secretary read:

The Prime Minister has asked me to thank you for your letter of 6 May. It was a kind thought and a great encouragement to her. She has always been proud of those who serve the Crown, and of their families who so often have to bear the anxiety of separation. She is proud of those in the South Atlantic task force, and has asked me to send you her best wishes.

Probably of a standard format, I presumed, but nevertheless I was pleased to receive it.

Date: *6 June 1982, Sunday*
Place: *Estancia House, same bivvy*
Weather: *Wet, windy, miserable*
Anniversary of D Day 1944, I think.
    Received a letter from 10 Downing Street today in reply to mine.
    Trench foot is now common, 3 of my men are bedded down in the shed and others are suffering but hoping to be able to take part in the attack which is supposed to take place tomorrow night.

Date: *7 June 1982, Monday*
Place: *Estancia House*
Weather: *Bright day but raining now*
2350 hours: [7.30 p.m. local] *All the plans for the attack have changed, there is now a Divisional plan to take Stanley in one big offensive. 3 Para is to do a big raid on Longdon tomorrow night. Longdon is still our objective. Told that the enemy are moving*

115

troops to West Falkland to enforce a political decision to split the Islands, so we may have to fight for that as well.

One of our snipers shot a duck today and we ate it for tea.

Trench continues to improve and we plan an extension tomorrow.

D Company had a contact at Murrel Bridge last night and had to abandon some of their equipment.

The SAS are to do a raid on Stanley Airfield tonight and also trying to knock out the 155mm guns. Enemy Hercules have been flying in and out at night.

Enemy mines are a problem and are undetectable – there have been some injuries.

Made a briefing model today of the objective area.

The contact between a patrol of D (Patrol) Company and a large force of enemy soldiers, later known to have been Special Forces, took place near the Murrel Bridge in an area used by Patrol Company as a patrol base. The patrol spotted the Argentines as they approached and opened fire on them. After a short but intense firefight the patrol withdrew to safety without casualties, but they had to abandon some equipment, including a set of radio codes. Major Dennison was critical of the loss of the codes, because the signaller should have followed 'SOPs' – Standing Operational Procedures, which stated that the codes should always be carried on the man, not in equipment that he may have to ditch in an emergency.

As it became clear to us that our stay at Estancia might be much longer than we expected, so the camp began to take on a more permanent look as shelters were improved and grew in number. A shelter was dug for the civilians at the farm, to be used when 'Air Raid Warning Red' was given. A latrine was dug behind some gorse bushes, facing Estancia Mountain and overlooking the tidal waters of the inlet. The primitive convenience consisted of a long trench spanned by a plank that was capable of seating four or five men at a time, perhaps more in an emergency. Although the view from the seat was a pleasant one when the sun was shining, it was nothing in comparison to one that I recalled using on a hillside during Battalion training in Sudan, which had allowed unobscured contemplation of a desert panorama to a distance of at least twenty miles. On one of my visits to the Estancia latrine I found that I shared the plank with the Battalion Padre, Derek Heaver (known as 'Derek the Cleric'). I had always felt uncomfortable in the presence of padres, finding it difficult to know what to say to them, and our precarious perch above the pit did nothing to help the conversation. After the customary greetings the Padre ventured, 'Do you think you could live here?' and I replied, 'Yes, but I'd prefer more trees.'

My attitude to the presence of padres in the front line was an arrogant one – if they could not fire a weapon then they were a waste of rations (I also included members of the press in the same category). I could understand that for the very few religious men that I knew the padre might add a sort religious legality to the killing, but for the rest of us he was unnecessary. I have since modified my opinion and I now believe that a padre is the only man on the battlefield who is free to show his true feelings and as such he is the only connection with a sane world and therefore able to achieve some empathy with the severely wounded. The rest of us instinctively wore masks and acted the parts allocated to us. A padre is more useful, though, if he is well trained as a medic.

Date: *8 June 1982, Tuesday*
Place: *Estancia*
Weather: *A good day, raining now*
2320 hours: [7.20 p.m. local] *Big improvements to the dug-out today – I am now sleeping in a bedroom behind the fire. We now have a large seat, a table, a new, smaller fire – with a better chimney, plus rifle racks and shelves.*

Mail arrived – received a Union Jack . . . and several yards of bunting! Also slides taken on Ascension.

As usual sporadic artillery fire, mainly outgoing – although no fire has reached this far west. A few air raid red alerts today – several Harriers seen flying in pairs. Chris Howard is out on the night raid on Longdon – he has taken a firing post with him.

The Harriers were the first friendly aircraft I had seen since the day we had cross-decked from *Canberra* to *Intrepid*. I had been surprised to receive my developed photographs in the mail; I had posted the film from the *Canberra* to the UK, giving the developers the address

117

of my barracks in Tidworth – from where it had been forwarded to me in the Falklands. It was proof of a very efficient postal system, but I would rather not have had to carry the pictures with me.

Chris had taken a firing post with him on the intended night raid, together with two men who carried missiles. They returned before dawn; Chris was in a foul mood, crying, 'Gutless Bastard!' among other things, because although the large force taking part in the raid had reached their fire positions unobserved, and some men had got close to the enemy positions, the commander had not given the order to open fire. We had understood that the mission of the large fighting patrol had been to engage the enemy on Mount Longdon and provoke return fire that would reveal the positions of their main weapons.

The Union Jack that I received came in a parcel that caused much merriment – I had collapsed with helpless laughter on the floor of the dugout as I pulled yard after yard of red, white and blue bunting from it – like handkerchiefs from a magician's hat. I erected a pole at the side of our home and tied the Union Jack to it, alongside a sign that I had made from a plank of wood with the following letters burned into it, 'RUMOUR CONTROL HQ'. Our luxurious accommodation had constant hot water boiling in the Argentine pot, and our meals were always supplemented with the captured rice. I liked our issued 'Arctic' rations, particularly the porridge and the drinking chocolate. Each box of rations, designed to last 24 hours, came with 'hexamine' solid-fuel blocks with which to heat water and food. The small white blocks of fuel were used in a tiny metal cooker carried by each man, on which a mess tin or metal mug would be placed. It was a simple but remarkably efficient heating method. There were rarely any inter-ruptions to our ration supply, but during one such period rationing of the available supplies was done by organised feeding at the barn, where we would go with our mess tins to collect a meagre portion of weak broth and a quarter of a bar of chocolate.

On 9 June we heard that the Welsh Guards had suffered 50 casualties on the LSL *Sir Galahad* when it was hit during an Argen-tine air attack at Bluff Cove. Two Mirages and Two Skyhawks were said to have been shot down in the raid. The involvement of 5 Infantry Brigade (with 2 Para now attached to it) was considered by us to be the cause of unnecessary delays – we felt that we had enough troops in 3 Commando Brigade to take Port Stanley, as I believe was subsequently proved. Although the Scots Guards were later to attack Mount Tumbledown, that could have been done by 40 Commando who instead were wasted in reserve back at San Carlos.

I was annoyed at the loss of three of my 19 men due to trench foot – a high proportion – and wondered if there was more I could have done to prevent it. I theorised that it may have been caused by the relative lack of marching that my men had done in comparison to most of the Battalion; we had flown from Port San Carlos to Teal and then spent long periods riding behind a tractor, whereas the rifle companies may have actually benefited from the long hours of marching which was an aid to blood circulation in the feet. I read an account afterwards of men of the 6th Airborne Division who, during the advance from Normandy to the Baltic when out of action had been made to run barefoot through snow in order to prevent the onset of trench foot.

A fourth man in my section told me that he had trench foot and wanted to see the Medical Officer. I took the man – a young lad actually, not yet twenty – to the farmhouse where the Battalion MO held his surgery, and an examination of his feet proved that he was in better condition than others who were determined not to see the doctor in case they missed the forthcoming attack. I suspected him of malingering and told him that he was OK and to return to his trench; he responded angrily with an insolent remark that caused me to lose my temper and attempt to punish him by knocking him around the room. Fortunately the doctor and a medic were quick to intervene – I was pulled away and sent outside, through another room where several Islanders wore concerned faces – they had heard the com-motion. I waited at the farmhouse gate and I had calmed down a little by the time the soldier made his appearance; I then told him, 'You will take part in the attack!' He agreed. The regrettable incident was perhaps a sign of a growing tension and frustration due to the delay in getting to grips with the enemy. I was relieved that no more of my men complained about their feet after that day.

Rumour Control HQ was a magnet for visitors. Some came, allegedly, because they had heard about the letter from Number Ten and wanted to see it, but most came because they knew about the fire and the constant availability of 'brews'. A better sign for our trench might have been, CORNER CAFÉ. The reporters Robert Fox and Max Hastings visited us with Colonel Pike on 10 June. Hastings took a photograph of the Commanding Officer standing next to the sign and my Union Jack. We had stuck the broken handle of our large spade in the ground as an aid to climbing out of the hole – Fox amused us by calling it a boot scraper.

The day of the Commanding Officer's visit was clear and sunny. Two Harriers flew past us in the morning. Coming in low and fast from the sea they sped over Estancia House in the direction of Port Stanley, causing a false 'Air Raid Red' warning to be sounded. Had they taken the same route at first light that day they would have interrupted four Argentine Pucara aircraft as they attacked our forward trenches – there were no casualties.

Preparations for our attack continued. As well as caring for the Milan firing posts and missiles, we stripped and oiled our rifles, sub-machine-guns and magazines. I used some of the Argentine ammunition to supplement my own. I loaded my rifle magazines with ten tracer and ten armour-piercing rounds each. I carried a total of 200 rounds of 7.62mm ammunition and two high explosive grenades, and hoped that my bayonet would not be necessary.

On Friday, 11 June, Major Dennison gave his orders for the attack on Mount Longdon to the assembled Support Company fire teams and attached ammunition bearers. We stood in an arc around the relief model I had made of the area and the key positions were pointed out to us. Patrol Company had obtained information about the Argentine dispositions on Longdon as a result of their intensive patrolling – several times their patrols had actually penetrated the enemy defences. This seemed to indicate a remarkably inefficient defensive system, and led to an assumption that the Argentine infantry unit there would soon give way under the pressure of our attack. There was confident talk of going on from Longdon to take Wireless Ridge and continuing eastwards from there all the way to Navy Point. Sergeant John Pettinger from Patrol Company described what he knew of the main enemy weapons and their locations, including a 120mm mortar and a command post. I was disappointed that there were no air photographs of the objective – our maps showed no detail – but I assumed that our pilots had had more important missions to fly.

120

Mount Longdon is a rocky ridge stretching, between its lower slopes, almost two kilometres from west to east, which was the direction chosen for the attack. The Argentines were known to have protected their position by minefields but they were unmarked (contrary to the Geneva Convention), so we did not know exactly where the mines lay. Major Dennison gave us the disturbing news that, in an attempt to achieve surprise, our attack would be 'silent', which is to say that there would be no preliminary 'softening up' of the enemy by artillery or any other weapons prior to the attack, which would only turn 'noisy' when our advancing troops were discovered by the enemy. The only disadvantage of a 'noisy' attack would have been that it might give away our intentions and alert the enemy. But the lesson learned by 2 Para at Goose Green, so we had been told, was that firepower was the key to success. It would appear that the successful patrolling of D Company had led to the opinion that a preliminary bombardment would be unnecessary. Well – we would soon find out.

9. BATTLE

To the junior leader himself the mere fact of responsibility brings courage; the mere fact that by his position as the recognised head of a group of men he is responsible for their lives and comfort, gives him less time to think of his own fears and so brings him a greater degree of resolution than if he were not the leader.

Field Marshal Bernard Montgomery, *The Path to Leadership*

———— • ◆ • ————

It was dry and sunny at noon on 11 June when a Wessex helicopter arrived at Estancia House and ferried the Support Company fire-support teams forward to the reverse slope of a hill near A Company's defensive position. It was a relief to be making a positive move after 11 nights of stagnation in the same area. The Milan missiles were brought up by tractor and delivered to us, followed by a reserve of missiles and some of the machine-gun ammunition which arrived on a sledge towed by a strange-looking vintage tractor on caterpillar tracks. This odd but effective contraption, driven by a farmer wearing a waxed jacket and flat cap, presented a most incongruous sight as it chugged along belching smoke and churning up the earth. The vehicle, which I never saw again, was to follow us forward to our objective once 45 Commando's objective, Two Sisters, was captured the same night. It was accompanied by various other civilian vehicles and Bandwagons which carried mortar bombs and the Battalion's reserve of small arms ammunition. The Blues and Royals with their light tanks would not accompany us this time, as they were still attached to 5 Infantry Brigade.

My fire team, after the reorganisation, consisted of seven men plus myself, and comprised a Milan firing post with a three-man crew led by Lance Corporal 'Stretch' Dunn, an SF machine-gun team of three men, and Phil Heyward with his sniper rifle. I also had eight men in

tow from HQ Company who were attached to our team as ammunition bearers and carried 600 extra machine-gun rounds each. These
men were designated as stretcher-bearers once the ammunition belts
they carried had been delivered to the guns at their fire positions.
There were two other fire teams, led by Captain Mason and Colour
Sergeant Steve 'Shakespeare' Knights, each with a mixture of two
Milan firing posts and two SF machine-guns.

We waited for darkness to begin our advance towards Mount
Longdon, and I took advantage of the time to rehearse the method of
occupying fire positions that I planned to use when we arrived at the
designated site to the west of the objective. I also took my men to a
spot near the crest of the hill and pointed Mount Longdon out to
them, which at a distance of about ten kilometres looked rather
insignificant and unthreatening. It was about to become the scene of
the British Army's hardest fought battle for nearly thirty years.

Being a rugby player I had always thought of the game as the
nearest one could legally get in peacetime to the experience of battle,
and in fact it has many similarities; two sides of men trained both as
individuals and as teams, with agreed and rehearsed tactics for the
trial ahead. The captains brief their men beforehand, and finish with
a few inspiring words before the teams assume their positions on the
field. Before the whistle, there is the nervous anticipation as each
player mentally rehearses his role in the coming clash of bodies, and
when battle is joined each team's strengths and weaknesses become
apparent. There will be acts of individual skill and clumsy mistakes;
and there will be the brave and the not so brave. There will even be
men within each team who deliberately or mistakenly break the rules
of the game. At times a team will lose its cohesiveness and give
ground to superior teamwork or greater strength. And then there
will always be an element of luck. Victory will not necessarily go to
the side with the best plan or the strongest team, but often to the
side that possesses that most intangible asset, team spirit. Morale.
Ésprit de Corps. The side that will stubbornly continue the fight in
the face of what seems like certain defeat and by sheer persistence
and self-belief reverse an apparently hopeless situation and triumph.
The analogy is a good one if one disregards the fact that battle has
few rules and no referee.

General Patton said to his men before the Sicily landings in 1943,

'Battle is the most magnificent competition in which a human being can indulge.'

Our team captain, Major Dennison, gathered us together in a circle and gave his team talk. Our group included two journalists who were to accompany us during the attack: Tom Smith and Les Dowd. Smith was a photographer for the *Daily Express*, and Dowd was a Reuters correspondent. The news was broken to us that one of the SAS observation posts had witnessed a reinforcement of Mount Longdon during the afternoon. The estimated strength of the enemy was a battalion and a half. This sobering intelligence (which fortunately proved to be an over estimate) seemed likely to prompt alterations to the plan of attack, but we learned that there were to be no changes – the attack would remain 'silent' with no preliminary bombardment of the enemy positions.

Had the enemy learned of our intentions? It seemed likely that such a large reinforcement of our objective only hours before our impending attack was more than just clever chess play on the part of the enemy commander, but of course we hoped that it was just coincidence. The idea that there could be a thousand soldiers or more on Mount Longdon, all awake and ready to open fire on us from their prepared positions was one which I avoided thinking about.

While we digested this new information we heard the whistle of an incoming shell, and I quickly made a decision to remain standing even though I had no idea how close it would land. The rest of our group had more sense and as the whistle increased in volume and pitch the men in the circle threw themselves to the ground as I held my defiant stand. The shell burst harmlessly in open ground about two hundred metres away to the north, and embarrassed laughter followed as men picked themselves up. My stand proved nothing, and I did it only to avoid the indignity of cowering in the face of what I recklessly hoped would be a distant explosion. As a boy I was often late for school because I would never run to catch a bus, and so avoided the indignity of arriving out of breath as the bus pulled away without me; I would walk calmly towards a bus which I knew was about to depart, and pretend unconcern when I missed it. This rather odd and illogical attitude to catching buses had similarities to the refusal to throw myself ignominiously to the ground to avoid possible death. During the following three days I modified my behaviour somewhat, and tempted fate less; my survival instinct took over and I did my fair share of ground-hugging, but on the 11 June I was still strolling calmly towards the bus stop.

The bright sunshine and an almost clear sky foretold a cold night to come. We spent the last minutes before dark talking in small groups. There was a surprisingly calm and cheerful atmosphere, everyone seemed confident, despite the predicted odds. It was a confidence that resulted from experience and training, and from the strong belief that we were superior to the opposition. I took some photographs and had some taken of me, imagining as I posed for the camera that my relatives would one day pass the photograph to visitors and say, 'This is the last photograph taken of him before he died.'

I made final adjustments to my equipment. I had a backpack radio with a metal frame and shoulder straps. I had strapped a Milan missile to the frame below the radio, which made an uneven-looking load due to the missile container's centre of gravity, which meant that more of it protruded from one side than the other. As I said earlier, the missiles were supposed to be subject to an RF, or radio frequency hazard, which in theory meant that nearby radio transmissions could cause the rocket motor, which propelled the missile to its target, to ignite. I had a humorous, cartoon-like vision in my mind of myself as a rocket-propelled soldier, flying around the battlefield strapped to my flaming missile.

I carried my rifle ammunition loaded in magazines in my webbing pouches and my smock pockets, and I also had a reserve of 50 rounds in five-round clips in a canvas bandolier slung across my chest. As well as the ammunition and two high explosive grenades I also carried two water bottles, several bars of chocolate, some biscuits and a brew kit in my webbing. I also wore binoculars around my neck, and carried my camera, spare film and diary in my pockets. My Union Jack was folded inside my smock, and I had an empty sandbag in which I planned to collect any interesting loot. My red beret I kept inside my helmet.

As the sky darkened we lifted our various loads and assembled in our formations ready for the advance. A three-hour march ahead of us stood Mount Longdon with its features nicknamed 'Free Kick', 'Fly Half' and 'Full Back'. The ultimate game was about to kick off.

My team were at the tail of the Support Company column, which

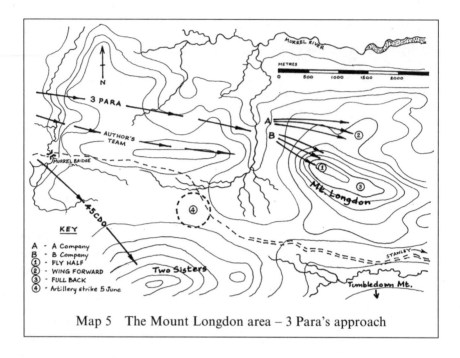

Map 5   The Mount Longdon area – 3 Para's approach

consisted of the three fire teams plus ammunition bearers and Company Headquarters, a total of around seventy men plus the forward RAP (Regimental Aid Post – the first point to which casualties would be taken for treatment prior to evacuation to the field hospital). A, B and C Companies were now hidden by the darkness somewhere to our north; B Company were the closest formation to our column and would advance on a parallel route to our left, led by men of Patrol Company who had been to Mount Longdon and were acting as guides. On our right, 45 Commando were to the south of us on the other side of the track running east towards Port Stanley, and they would attack the Two Sisters feature, while to their right 42 Commando would attack Mount Harriet. 2 Para, now returned to 3 Commando Brigade from Fitzroy where they had been under command of 5 Infantry Brigade, were to follow up and be ready to support either ourselves or 45 Commando.

For some reason we were not made aware of, 45 Commando's attack on Two Sisters was not due to begin until one hour after the start of our attack on Mount Longdon, even though their objective was nearly two kilometres closer than ours – I assume this was because our attack was to be 'silent', and an attack on Two Sisters would have alerted the Longdon defenders. The difference in start times meant that 3 Para would advance towards Mount Longdon with our right flank exposed to the enemy on Two Sisters, which lay almost two kilometres to the south of the planned route of the Support Company fire teams. The enemy on Two Sisters were of little concern to us, however, and I was pleased to note that 3 Para were once again to be the most advanced unit in the Brigade, and once we were on Mount Longdon, would be the closest British unit to Port Stanley.

Our greatest concerns during the advance were firstly the possibility of bumping into enemy patrols (although from the Argentinian tactics so far there appeared to be only a small chance of this); secondly the risk of walking into a minefield (although our patrols on previous nights had not suffered any mine casualties); and thirdly the danger that our advance would be detected by enemy observation aided by night-vision devices or parachute flares, and that artillery, mortar and other support weapons would then be fired in our direction. What the enemy might do to us when we finally came within small arms range of Mount Longdon was not an immediate problem, and would be dealt with when the time came.

We were to advance in company columns in single file, or as it was colloquially known, 'company snake'. Single file is a good formation for control at night, but has disadvantages; enemy fire from the front or rear can quickly cause many casualties, and a large number of men in single file can make for a very long line, making movement at night over long distances difficult, particularly for those at the rear. The 'snake' seems to take on a life of its own, contracting and extending in various parts as it advances. The need, particularly at night, to pause for navigation checks, to cross obstacles or to rest tends to make the line close up as each man realises that the man ahead, who he is trying to keep a reasonable distance from to avoid bunching, has stopped. When the lead man starts to tab again, there is a natural stretching of the line, and by the time the last man gets up from his temporary fire position he finds himself hurrying to catch up.

When it was fully dark, at around 4.30 p.m., the advance began. We had nine kilometres of open ground to cover to our first fire positions that were to be just short of a stream that was the designated Start Line for the attack, nicknamed, 'Free Kick', 800 metres from the summit of Mount Longdon. Such nicknames were allocated as a simple code for use during radio conversations. A and B companies were due to cross the Start Line at 8.01 p.m. and we had to be in position to support them before that time. Three and a half hours to cover the nine kilometres ought to have been ample time, even allowing for the crossing of the Murrel River that flowed from south to north across our line of advance three kilometres short of the Start Line, but unforeseen problems – 'the friction of war' – were to impose delays. Soon after the advance began, as we were crossing the top of the first of the low hills on our route, I received a radio message from Major Dennison instructing me to check the vehicles to see if any carried the 'special equipment'. If codes or nicknames were not used in radio voice procedure, then we used what was known as 'veiled speech' to camouflage the meaning to the enemy who may have been listening, tuned to the same frequency. I had no idea what the special equipment might be, but assumed that it would be apparent if I saw it. I halted my team and returned to the vehicles, which had not yet begun to advance. I could find nothing but ammunition and so reported a negative finding to the Company Commander. It later transpired that the 'special equipment' was a steel girder that was being carried to bridge the Murrel River and so avoid a wet crossing. Had I been asked to look for a steel girder, then the meaning would have been clear to me and it would probably have puzzled the enemy.

The rifle companies were to cross the river on a bridge of ladders provided by 9 Squadron, the Para Engineers, but at a crossing point further to our north. In the meantime the Company snake had continued to advance, and when I returned to my team I found them separated from the teams in front, which I could not see or hear. The moon had not risen at that time, which gave us cover from the enemy but at the same time restricted our own vision. I took out my compass on which I had earlier set a bearing which would take me directly towards Mount Longdon and my fire positions, and resumed the tab, hoping to catch up with the Company. I knew that if I did not, I would be able to find my own way to my allocated position on the Start Line, having seen it during our recce patrol six nights previously. Despite increasing the pace of our advance I could not find

The author in the Sergeants' Mess at Kandahar Barracks, Tidworth, with the Forecast of Events board.

The Anti-tank Platoon assemble on the parade ground at Kandahar Barracks prior to departure for Southampton.

Southampton docks – Canberra's forward heli-deck under construction.

Heading south. Colour-Sergeant Dave 'Scoop' McGachen on *Canberra*. A Sea King helicopter sits on the mid-ships heli-deck, which was formerly a swimming pool.

A Milan crew pose for press photographs on board *Canberra* with a lion mascot and a model tank flying an Argentine flag. The Milan firing post is loaded with a dummy ammunition 'tube', which if live would contain a missile. When fired, the force of the launched missile would cause the tube to be ejected rearwards from the firing post. The 'Number One', here seen looking into the weapon sight, would fire the missile and control its flight by adjusting his aim until it struck its target. The 'Number Two' would load the ammunition tubes onto the firing post.

Training on Ascension Island. SF machine-gun firing and (below) an 81mm mortar crew in action.

Ascension Island. Wombat 120mm anti-tank guns being fired across the volcanic landscape at 'Wideawake Fairs'.

After a day of training on Ascension Island, men of 3 Para queue for landing craft that will return them to the *Canberra*.

On board *Canberra*, with HMS *Fearless* in the background. The Milan Section of 3 Para with their Milan firing posts. Three of the men were killed on Mount Longdon: Corporal 'Ginge' McCarthy (*7th from right*), Private Pete Hedicker (*8th from right*) and Private Phil West (*11th from right*). Corporal Mick Mathews (*4th from right*) was killed by Irish terrorists in Ulster six years later. (*Photographed by the author.*)

D-Day, 21 May 1982. 3 Para arrive at Port San Carlos by landing craft. *(Top)* Approaching land in a LCU and *(below)* C Company and the Milan Section disembark at 'Green Two'. A Scorpion light tank waits in the LCU behind the disembarking troops. Two LCVP can be seen in the background heading for 'Green One' (Sand Bay) at Port San Carlos Settlement. A Milan crew is in the foreground.

21 May. Sergeant Chris Howard at Windy Gap, celebrating a successful D-Day with a cigar. The Union Jack was given to the author before departing England. Two 66mm anti-tank rockets (LAW) are in the foreground.

The author shaving in his trench at Windy Gap.

29 May, Teal Inlet. The only British Chinook helicopter to make it to the Falklands – the rest were sunk with the *Atlantic Conveyor*. An Argentine prisoner is lying beneath the two kneeling HQ Company soldiers.

30 May. Some of the Milan Section departing Teal Inlet on a sledge towed by Dave Thorsen.

Windy Gap, looking towards 'Bomb Alley', San Carlos Water. A patrol leaves the B Company defensive position for the night.

Sunset at Windy Gap. Chris Howard has a 'Bren' light machine-gun magazine fitted to his rifle, holding 30 rounds rather than the usual 20.

31 May. 3 Para tab around the inlets towards Estancia House. Smoko Mount is in the distance, centre of horizon.

2 June. Estancia House – looking east in the direction of Stanley. A Scimitar *(left)* and a Scorpion of the Blues and Royals wait with civilian vehicles as a Sea King departs after delivering more ammunition. Mount Kent is in the distance between the two armoured vehicles.

3 June, Estancia House, prior to the aborted attack on Mount Longdon. The author and Phil Heyward with a sledge packed with Milan ammo, rations and equipment. Tony Heathman, the owner of Estancia House, is in the cluster of people, fifth from right, wearing wellingtons.

Sergeant Howard (left) and Corporal 'Ollie' Oliver stand in the garden of Estancia farmhouse. The 3 Para Battalion flag is flying beneath the flag of the Union.

1 June, Estancia House. Islanders watch as a Sea King releases its under-slung load. The trailer contains bergens belonging to the Milan Section, ready to be delivered to the forward positions on Estancia Mountain.

Sunshine at Estancia House, with Estancia Mountain behind. Ollie and Chris stand beside the author's Union Jack, flying above the 'Rumour Control HQ' dugout.

11 June. The Support Company fire teams board a Wessex bound for Battalion forward positions, prior to the advance on Mount Longdon.

Mount Longdon; the northern slope looking east. An enemy anti-tank missile is in the foreground.

The rocky northern slope of Mount Longdon; a British soldier looks west towards Mount Estancia.

The author at the assembly area forward of Estancia Mountain. Waiting for darkness to fall before advancing on Mount Longdon. The picture was taken looking northwest towards Teal Inlet which lies beyond the distant hills.

13 June, on Mount Longdon. Chris Howard firing a captured 12.7mm machine-gun.

After the surrender, looking west from an enemy artillery position near Stanley Racecourse. Moody Valley is the low ground in the centre distance. Mount Longdon and Wireless Ridge lie on the right (north) side of the valley; Two Sisters and Mount Tumbledown to the left.

Private 'Stretch' Dunn with his Milan firing post on Mount Longdon. Shrapnel holes are visible in the blast shield.

13 June, Mount Longdon. Argentine prisoners remove their dead from 'the bowl'.

12 June, Mount Longdon, near 'Fly Half'. Argentine dead at a command post. The soldier on the right is a prisoner replacing his jacket after being searched; he has a bandaged leg wound. Some of the Longdon defenders had been shot in the leg by their officers, in case they deserted their positions.

Mount Longdon, just north of 'the bowl'. The author (left) and Chris Howard
carry 12.7mm ammo to one of the captured machine-gun posts. There are
damaged Milan firing posts to their left.

Near the top of the west slope of Longdon, in an enemy 81mm mortar pit, the
author (left) holds a mortar bomb and Chris Howard holds a 105mm anti-tank
round. Mount Kent is in the centre distance.

The author's Union Jack on top of the sangar he occupied at the northern entrance to 'the bowl'. Sergeant Howard stands; Corporal Mathews is to his left.

The top of the ridge on Mount Longdon. Chris Howard and an enemy anti-tank gun.

Mount Longdon, photographed from the west, scene of B Company's initial attack.

12 June. Chris Howard looks down from the western summit of Mount Longdon, where four 3 Para men died; upturned rifles mark where they fell. Blankets cover the bodies.

13 June. Looking east along the top of the ridge of Mount Longdon towards 'Full Back' (the rocks to the left of the right-hand rifle), which was captured by A Company. Rifles mark the spot where Lance Corporal 'Doc' Murdoch of B Company and Private 'Geordie' Laing of the Anti-tank Platoon fell; this was the limit of B Company's advance. Port Stanley can be glimpsed in the distance, mid-way between the two rifles.

14 June. Beginning the last leg of an 8,000-mile journey to Port Stanley. Preparing to move, and (below) advancing along the northern slopes of Longdon towards Wireless Ridge. In the above picture, Steve 'Shakespeare' Knights is nearest the camera; the picture below shows Private Pat Harley in the foreground carrying a Milan missile.

14 June. Stretch Dunn's Milan Detachment and Phil Heyward pause at Moody Brook on their way into Stanley. An abandoned and partly camouflaged enemy Huey sits behind them.

14 June. The author at the western edge of Stanley, near the Racecourse. The pilot of the enemy Huey had just landed and surrendered.

The author with a Pucara on Stanley airfield.

Members of the Anti-tank Platoon with an Argentine 105mm howitzer to the west of Stanley. *Left to right:* Corporal Whittle, the author, Corporal Richardson, Lance Corporal Rowell. Sapper Hill can be seen to the rear.

Raising the author's Union Jack at Port Stanley.

Paratrooper graves at Teal Inlet.

any other troops, and I concentrated on maintaining direction, aware of the possibility of a chance encounter with enemy patrols.

Ahead of us and to the right lay Two Sisters, which began to be pounded by our artillery, adding drama to the occasion, but doing nothing to increase our confidence; our objective, at this stage still at least a two-hour march ahead of us, waited silently in the gloom. I began to feel the familiar aches of the foot soldier as the straps and belt of my heavy equipment dug into my shoulders and hips, and my ankles turned and twisted in the rough and boggy ground.

A gradual descent took us down towards the Murrel River and the scene of the skirmish five nights earlier between D Company patrols and a strong enemy patrol. I became cautious on the approach to the river, looking for signs of enemy on the higher ground beyond, and at the same time searching for a suitable crossing point. This would have been an ideal area for the enemy to deploy early warning or ambush parties. The obvious crossing point was the Murrel Bridge, about four hundred metres to our right, and therefore we avoided it in case it was mined or ambushed. I found a point on the riverbank where the crossing appeared easiest and returned to my halted team to bring them forward. My waterproof trousers had been torn some days earlier, but I had kept the two legs and tied a knot in the bottom of each one, intending to pull them over my boots as extra defence against the wet and cold. I used them now, and waded through the river at a surprisingly shallow point. I climbed up the bank at the far side before discarding my improvised over-boots and congratulated myself on remaining reasonably dry. I then moved forward to wait and give cover for the remainder of my men to cross, and as I did so I sank to my thighs in boggy ground. By the time I had extricated myself and found some reasonably solid ground I was so wet that I felt as though I had just crawled through the river.

When all of my team had crossed and received their various soakings, I checked my watch and realised that if we were to be in position on time then I would have to increase the pace of the tab, which I did as we climbed on to the long, low hill that extended towards our destination. It was from this feature that we had called artillery fire down on to the enemy trucks in the valley to the south during our recce patrol. As we climbed towards the crest of the hill I was suddenly immobilised by an attack of cramp in my thigh, and before I was able to continue a whispered message was passed to me – two of the ammunition bearers were lagging behind. I could not afford to wait, and resumed the march without them, hoping that they would catch up later. In fact the two men did not reunite with us until we were on the summit of Mount Longdon, where they delivered their loads to the gun teams and went to the rear to report as stretcher-bearers.

Two Sisters was now to our right, and we, being the southernmost fire team, the closest 3 Para men to it. I was prepared to deploy my weapons and engage the hill if we received fire from it. The hill was within Milan range and at the limit of the range of the SF gun, but we were untroubled as I continued to force the pace and keep an eye on the time. I was unaware of the movements of the remainder of the Battalion to my left, but it turned out that the river crossing had taken longer than expected, and Captain Mason, who was leading the Support Company column (minus my own team) had wandered off to the north and cut through the B Company platoons, causing 5 and 6 Platoons to become separated. B Company eventually managed to reunite but there had been a 20-minute delay. At this time I was probably, although unaware of the honour, the furthest forward man in 3 Para, and therefore in the Brigade.

At last we reached the eastern end of the low hill where the ground fell away gradually towards the stream and our intended positions. The silhouette of Mount Longdon loomed dark and menacing ahead of us. It was only minutes before 8 p.m., and I decided to abandon the cautious plan we had rehearsed for occupying the fire positions, and instead moved all of the team forward at once. We deployed with the Milan firing post on the left and the machine-gun to the right, I lay with my sniper between the Milan firing post, now with a missile loaded on to it, and the tripod-mounted machine-gun. With only three minutes to spare before the 8.01 p.m. deadline, I reported to Major Dennison by radio and informed him that I was in position. There was no cover from enemy fire; we lay behind small ledges of peat and tried to convince ourselves that we had some protection, but we were so much lower than the enemy positions that we were completely exposed to any fire that might come from them.

My wet legs and feet, and the sweat on my back caused by the exertion of the last hour, meant that I felt most uncomfortable in the freezing temperature. I had been told that the other fire teams were late but I did not know that A and B companies would not cross the Start Line for a further 20 minutes due to the problems that had delayed them on the advance. We lay and shivered in our exposed positions, hoping that the enemy were asleep and that they would not put up parachute flares – had they done so it would have made visible the whole of our Battalion deployed below them. I strained to see the enemy and the advancing B Company through my binoculars, with no success. I could make out small dark shapes near the summit that could have been sangars, but on the other hand may just have been rocks. The machine-gun team had an IWS (Individual Weapon Sight) but that did not help much. The only other type of night viewing aid with the Support Company fire teams was an image-intensifier called NOD (Night Observation Device) with our Sergeant-Major, Thor Caithness. Not for the last time that night, I wished that I had a Thermal Imager like the ones I had used during trials not long before we left England.

We were facing the western side of Mount Longdon, which happened to be the steepest and led up to the summit, from which point the top of the long ridge extended away from us towards the east, dropping slightly into a long saddle before rising again to another, lower peak 600 metres beyond the summit. From the lower peak there was a gradual descent further eastwards for another two kilometres before the ground began to rise up towards Wireless Ridge, which would be A Company's objective, if B Company was successful on Mount Longdon. The dominating height of Mount Longdon was a problem for us until we closed with the enemy on it; but what added to the difficulty was the rocky nature of the ground. This was no smoothly rounded hill such as the ones we were used to attacking in training exercises on Salisbury Plain and elsewhere, but a jagged, uneven ridge which was covered, especially on the northern slopes, by masses of rocks which not only gave cover for the defenders but would have made a coordinated advance up and along it almost impossible in daylight, never mind in darkness.

The plan called for Major Mike Argue's B Company to assault towards the summit, nicknamed 'Fly Half', and then to fight forward along the ridge to the second peak, 'Full Back'. A Company, led by Major Dave Collet, would advance to B Company's left, on the

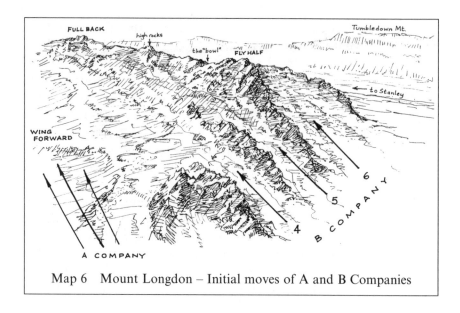

Map 6   Mount Longdon – Initial moves of A and B Companies

northern side of the hill, and occupy 'Wing Forward', a spur of high ground running north from the centre of the ridge, from where they would be ready to move forward to Wireless Ridge. C Company under Major Martin Osborne was to be held in reserve. The rifle companies were each reinforced by extra men with 84mm Carl Gustav launchers and GPMGs from the Wombat Section of the Anti-tank Platoon. As well as the Support Company fire teams of five Milan firing posts and five SF machine-guns, plus a .30 inch Browning machine-gun of 9 Para Squadron Royal Engineers, the Mortar Platoon with six 81mm 'tubes' would be 'on call', positioned back near the Murrel River. In addition the Battalion had available an artillery battery of six 105mm Light Guns from 29 Commando Regiment, and Naval Gunfire Support in the form of the 4.5 inch gun of the frigate HMS *Avenger*. Advancing with B Company Head-quarters was a two-man NGFO team from 148 Battery Royal Artillery, consisting of Captain Willie McCracken and a signaller. It was their job to request and control the fire from the frigate, which was somewhere to the north of the Islands.

The three platoons and headquarters of B Company would be moving across in front of us from our left, and then advancing

164

straight forward up the hill. Because we could not see the advancing troops I knew that there was little chance of us firing either the Milan or the machine-gun unless B Company requested it, and they were advancing up the steep slope ahead of us so we would have to fire over their heads. The closer they got to the enemy the more dangerous our fire would become to them.

B Company was advancing with 4 Platoon left, 5 Platoon centre and 6 Platoon right, commanded respectively by Lieutenants Bickerdike, Cox and Shaw. Guided by Sergeant Pettinger's men from Patrol Company and followed by Company Headquarters they were around a hundred and twenty strong. Major Argue's unorthodox plan called for 6 Platoon to attack from west to east, until halfway along the ridge. 4 and 5 Platoons would advance along the northern edge of the ridge to the halfway point, then move up to the centre of the ridge to take over from 6 Platoon and attack towards Full Back. We were told that the enemy had concentrated most of his positions at the eastern end of the ridge around Full Back, but in fact this was not the case – there was a spread of defensive sangars all the way along the northern slope for about seven hundred metres.

6 Platoon had managed to advance undetected up on to the summit, Fly Half, when a loud explosion and a scream off to their left alerted the dozing Argentines. Corporal Milne, leading his section on the left of 4 Platoon to the north of the ridge, had stepped on a mine, and the battle commenced. I checked my watch as the hill banged and crackled to life – it was 9.10 p.m.

———— •◆• ————

The firing was slow and sporadic at first, and it was still impossible for us to observe any targets from our fire positions below the western slopes of the ridge. In fact I was unaware that B Company had already advanced too far for me to support them from my current position. There was the occasional flash as a grenade exploded or a 66mm or 84mm rocket was fired, and some lines of tracer sped around in all directions, but there appeared to be no enemy fire coming from anywhere on the western slope of the hill; instead the main resistance appeared to be situated beyond the crest to the east, indicating that B Company were already at the top. An occasional distant yell or scream could be heard between the explosions and gunfire. My radio was tuned to the Support Company fire control net, which remained strangely silent. Had I been tuned to the B Company frequency I would have been fully aware of the chaotic nature of their struggle to advance through the deadly maze of rocks; instead I remained blissfully ignorant and assumed that the attack was proceeding as planned.

Assuming that we would not be called on to fire from this position, I awaited instructions to move forward in support of B Company and their continuing fight along the ridge, but instead I was ordered to move to the north and RV with Support Company Headquarters. I duly moved towards the north but I could not see anybody, so I used my radio to ask for a torch to be flashed in my direction, and located a small group of men behind a bank of peat on slightly higher ground. Major Dennison was with Sergeant-Major Caithness and the two reporters. I was told that Captain Mason's team had been sent forward to support A Company, who had advanced on the left of B Company towards Wing Forward, and that Shakespeare's team had moved towards B Company with the Regimental Aid Post and some stretcher-bearers.

During a further wait, the Reuters reporter, Les Dowd, asked me if Mount Longdon was a position I would like to defend. I answered to the effect that if 3 Para held it then more than a battalion would be needed to capture it.

Finally, Major Dennison decided to move us forward to support the attack along the ridge from Fly Half to Full Back. We moved over Free Kick, the stream that had been the Start Line, through what we later discovered to be a minefield, and climbed across the western slope of Mount Longdon to a small group of rocks where the Regimental Aid Post had been established. From one of the medics there we learned that B Company had taken heavy casualties, and some of the wounded were stuck in the open where attempts to rescue them had resulted in more men killed and wounded.

We continued to trudge up the hill past small groups of enemy prisoners who were being escorted down. I was surprised to see this. I did not believe that it could be safely ascertained whether a man was surrendering in the darkness and confusion of the ongoing battle.

My men and I struggled upwards past the ends of the long lines of rock slabs that were a distinctive feature of the north-western side of the hill, and then turned left up the western slope towards the top. This had been the route taken by 6 Platoon earlier. As we ascended, heavy machine-gun fire crackled harmlessly over our heads from enemy guns somewhere to the east along the ridge. It was easy to tell that it was safe to continue upwards because the lines of tracer flew above us and sped over the area of our earlier advance from the Murrel River. I passed Private Harley from Shakespeare's fire team on his way to the top; he was struggling upwards with two Milan missiles so I took one from him and carried it to where the Support Company Milan and machine-gun teams were assembling in an area of abandoned enemy sangars a short distance from the crest, which was still being raked by enemy fire. This was to be Major Dennison's Headquarters location throughout the battle. There were some B Company men from 6 Platoon in this area, although most of B Company were then forward and to the left of us, grouped mainly on the northern slope of the hill which, because it was more undulating and rocky, offered more cover. But the majority of the Argentine positions had been established on that same northern slope. Captain Mason's fire team was still with A Company further to the left of B Company down below us.

I unstrapped the missile from my backpack ready for possible use. I was eager to deploy my weapons to suppress the enemy fire, but the OC told me to wait for orders. I positioned myself alongside a substantial enemy sangar with a good roof of rocks, and although I assumed that it had been checked for enemy I decided to make sure and pulled back the waterproof material that hung over the entrance before crawling in with a torch held against my rifle with my left hand. With my right hand I removed my safety catch and prepared to pull the trigger. A pistol would have been less cumbersome and better for the task, and I have to admit that one of my reasons for searching inside was the possibility of acquiring one. The first thing I noticed was the smell of unwashed human bodies. A quick sweep with my torch revealed a spacious interior that could have accommodated at least six men. After satisfying myself that there were no enemy left inside I rummaged through the abandoned blankets and equipment. My first find was a control unit for a 'Cobra' anti-tank guided missile system which was positioned in the centre of a wide, deep slit which faced to the west and provided a good field of view down the face of the hill and beyond. The unit consisted of a joystick on a base with a telescope mounted above it, and cables connected to the base ran forward through the slit, presumably to the missiles. I also found a plastic box which I was pleased to see contained a set of night-vision goggles. I crawled out of the sangar and rejoined the team outside. Rifle and machine-gun fire still crackled over us but it was less intense than before. High-velocity rounds make a loud crack when they pass by, breaking the sound barrier. The Argentines used the same 7.62mm calibre rounds as us in their rifles and machine-guns, but they were also firing several 12.7mm heavy machine-guns.

I fiddled around with the night-vision goggles and got them to work. I could clearly see the various sangars and emplacements around me, from which the enemy should have spotted us and opened fire well before we had gained a toehold on the hill. Subsequent Argentine accounts of the battle reveal that they were caught unawares by the attack, and some of their positions were quickly captured by B Company. It had been the men manning these positions who had become the first prisoners taken in the battle, the ones I had passed on the way up the hill. Had they been alert and used their night-vision goggles and the ground-surveillance radar, which was also positioned in the same area, the enemy ought to have been able, with the weapons and large quantities of ammunition at their disposal, to successfully defend Mount Longdon. It seemed as if they had not expected us to attack at night.

My captured night-vision goggles were of good quality, and I hung them around my neck on top of my binoculars, ready to use when we were called forward to the crest of the hill. B Company and the stretcher-bearers were attempting to evacuate their casualties back through 5 Platoon's area on the northern slopes to our left at that stage. I told Major Dennison that I thought we should have a go with Milan and he agreed. Chris Howard seemed to have attached himself to my fire team again and was as keen as ever to fire a missile. By the time I had returned from Company Headquarters, Chris had already 'borrowed' a firing post from one of the Milan teams. I decided to be his 'Number Two', and picked up a missile. We crawled forward to a suitable position on top of the ridge, and Chris levelled the firing post on its tripod. The cable of my radio caught around a rock and I could not reach to load the missile to the firing post, so I slid backwards to free myself. Chris had loaded the tube when I reached my position to the right of the post. The moon had risen to the east, which threw the large outcrops of rock into dark silhouette. There were two main areas of rocks to our front along the ridge: one was the eastern high feature, Full Back, and there was another, closer group of high rocks to the left of it. I handed my night-vision goggles to Chris and he tried to spot the muzzle flashes of a sniper who we thought was probably firing from the closer rocks. It was impossible to estimate the range to the rocks, but it appeared to be beyond the missile's minimum range of 300 metres, so Chris aimed at the likely spot where he judged the sniper to be, and pressed the firing button. There was a tremendous flash and a much louder bang than there ought to have been. The missile launched but climbed high into the sky. The tube containing the missile, which was supposed to slide off the firing post to the rear, had split open, and some of the blast from the ignition of the missile's rocket motor had been directed sideways, blowing off the metal blast shield at the side of the firing post and striking Chris's helmet. I disconnected the control wire that had linked the fired missile to the firing post and we slid backwards from our exposed position, amazed that we had not been hit by enemy fire, especially since we had been illuminated by a bright flash when the missile was fired.

Chris collected another firing post and I picked up another missile before heading back to the summit for another go. This time the launch was successful and the missile flew to its target and exploded in the rocks, to what effect it was impossible to tell. Sniper fire continued. Private 'Mushrooms' Bateman of the Anti-tanks watched the missile as it flew over his head; as I was to learn from him later, he lay pinned down on top of the ridge, shot through the throat and therefore unable to call for help.

We now clung to the area of Fly Half, the western summit, and there was a pause in the battle until Colonel Pike coordinated the next attack. Having taken the most tactically important part of the ridge we could have held on to it, dominating the remaining enemy positions towards the east and not taking the risk of continuing our attack. The Argentines would have found it extremely difficult to hold their remaining positions in daylight – but that plan would not have occurred to any of us, it was not the Airborne way – our mission was to capture Mount Longdon by first light – and that meant all of it.

During several hours of fighting B Company had been severely mauled and were now in no shape to continue their planned attack to capture the remaining part of the ridge, including the strong enemy position around Full Back. Despite the early mine explosion which had alerted the Argentines, the attack had initially progressed well; 5 Platoon, advancing through the rocks on the northern slope, had taken the first enemy fire and some casualties. 6 Platoon, advancing on the right of B Company and climbing straight up the western face, had also made good progress through enemy sangars and tents and along the top of the ridge which had appeared to be deserted, until the mine explosion down to the north of them had sparked the enemy fire to their left. Lieutenant Shaw had been advancing with an enlarged Headquarters of 12 men in the centre of his 6 Platoon behind 2 Section, which had passed Fly Half and was moving down the centre of the ridge. The Platoon Commander had lost visual contact with 3 Section to his left and 1 Section to his right. 3 Section, advancing on the high part of the northern slope with 5 Platoon down to their left, came under fire from enemy positions to their rear that they had missed during their advance and from positions to their front. To regain control of his Platoon and assist 3 Section, Lieutenant Shaw called his 1 and 2 Sections back to Fly Half. 2 Section withdrew without incident, but 1 Section, when they moved up to the top of the hill from the southern slope, was fired on and one man was hit. 1 Section then took another four casualties in quick succession as men went to help the injured. Lieutenant Shaw had to order his men to stop trying to reach the exposed casualties.

5 Platoon, further down to the left of 6 Platoon, had advanced beyond them, and were in danger from 6 Platoon's fire as they attempted to assist their 3 Section. 6 Platoon were therefore told to stop firing. Eventually, the men of 3 Section 6 Platoon were able to extract themselves and deal with the enemy to their rear, though not without loss.

4 Platoon on the left of B Company, their advance disrupted by the jagged rocks on the north side of the ridge, became mingled with the left of 5 Platoon, and while pushing forward with them along the northern slopes came under heavy fire and were pinned down, taking

casualties and forcing them further up the side of the ridge into cover.

Sergeant Ian McKay, who took command of 4 Platoon after the Platoon Commander, Lieutenant Bickerdike had been wounded, was killed leading a small group of men forward to deal with one of the enemy positions. For this brave act he was awarded the Victoria Cross. Similar acts of bravery by the men of B Company were not uncommon during the battle.

Sergeant Des Fuller was sent forward from B Company Headquarters to take over command of 4 Platoon. Leading an ad hoc force consisting of the remnants of 4 Platoon plus Corporal 'Scouse' McLaughlin's Section from 5 Platoon in an attempt to knock out a machine-gun, Sergeant Fuller had eventually been forced to withdraw after suffering more casualties. At this stage, with 6 Platoon pinned down on top of the ridge and 4 and 5 Platoons seemingly unable to advance, Major Argue decided to pull 4 and 5 Platoons back with their wounded, before calling in an artillery strike on the enemy positions that were holding up the attack. A heavy bombardment followed before another force was assembled from the remnants of 4 and 5 Platoons under Lieutenant Cox to continue the attack. This last assault by B Company was eventually broken up by heavy small arms and mortar fire, having progressed no further eastwards than the point they had reached before their OC had ordered their withdrawal. CSM Johnny Weeks had been the archetypal Company Sergeant-Major throughout these attacks – as steadfast as the huge rocks around him – rallying and encouraging the young paras of B Company by his example.

B Company's battle had not been the fluid, steadily advancing, 'Deliberate Attack' of the textbook that we all knew and had trained for; instead it had consisted of a confused succession of independent attacks by various sized groups of men. They had used grenade, rifle, machine-gun and shoulder-fired anti-tank weapons, as well as bayonets, to overcome enemy positions that were sometimes impossible to distinguish from the surrounding terrain. Supporting each other, and often dying for each other, the men of B Company had struggled for over six hours to gain their objective in the face of unexpectedly stubborn resistance. By the time the Commanding Officer decided to halt B Company they had suffered many casualties, but they had overcome a strong enemy to gain control of the area around Fly Half, which provided a platform to launch what would be the final attack by A Company to seize the remainder of the ridge.

From my position on Fly Half I could see, behind and to the right of me across the valley, 45 Commando's attack on Two Sisters. Further to the south but hidden from us by Mount Tumbledown, 42 Commando was attacking Mount Harriet.

Artillery, naval gunfire and mortars had eventually been used in support of B Company's attack on Mount Longdon, directed initially at the enemy depth positions around Full Back, but later it fell much closer to our own positions. Sometimes the fire was so close to us that it was impossible to tell our own gun and mortar fire from that of the enemy, until the 4.5 inch gun of HMS *Avenger* joined in with its regular shell bursts, a single explosion evenly spaced in time every couple of seconds, as opposed to the artillery fire which landed in groups of three or six shells. It was difficult to understand how a ship could deliver such accurate close supporting fire while forging through the waves several miles away, and it must have come close to causing casualties among us, but it was welcome.

During periods when the bombardment was heaviest it was impossible to communicate above the din, and there were other times when the battlefield fell eerily silent. In the lull before A Company began to attack we waited for orders and did our best to get warm. I wrapped an Argentine blanket, taken from one of the sangars, around my wet legs. My feet were numb and swollen and I took the only spare clothing I carried, a pair of socks, from my trouser pockets and temporarily pulled them over my toecaps for extra insulation.

Captain Mason's fire team rejoined us after supporting A Company down to the north. It included Cpl 'Ginge' McCarthy's Milan team. Ginge told me that he had fired two Milan missiles at enemy positions on the northern side of the ridge. Major Dennison returned from a meeting with the Commanding Officer and told us that it had been decided to pass Major Collet's A Company through B Company to continue the attack along the ridge to Full Back. We were to provide fire support for the attack, firing from positions along the crest at the top of Fly Half. A Company would attack from a position forward and to the left of us on the northern side of the ridge. They had suffered some casualties when they advanced to occupy exposed positions in peat banks on the Wing Forward feature, being overlooked by the enemy higher up on Mount Longdon to their south. They were pulled back from Fly Half before moving up behind B Company.

In preparation for our support of A Company's attack, the five SF machine-guns were deployed in a line across the crest, together with three Milan firing posts and a 'Bren' light machine-gun from 9 Para Squadron, Royal Engineers. My machine-gun was on the right of the line, and I found room to site Stretch Dunn's Milan post to the right of them. This deployment of the fire teams at the top of the hill near Fly Half was, in my opinion, long overdue. From these positions we could fire all the way along the top of the ridge as far as Full Back, the eastern summit. Ginge and his Milan crew were not deployed and remained behind us in dead ground below the crest.

There was an Argentine 105mm recoilless anti-tank gun near Full Back that had been causing problems. I told Stretch to take aim at what I thought was the gun emplacement, some six hundred metres away. I looked through his Milan sight to check the aim and asked Company Headquarters by radio for 'permission to open fire with Milan'. To my surprise, my request was refused. I then wished that I had ordered Stretch to fire without asking permission.

Sergeant-Major Caithness positioned himself with his Night Observation Device at the highest point in the line of weapons, and prepared to control and direct our fire on to Full Back. Eventually, A Company began to call for our support. The Sergeant-Major gave the order for the machine-guns to open fire, and after observing the lines of tracer, he gave corrections to their aim via the fire team commanders by radio, until all the SF guns were hitting the required targets.

The A Company Commander was apparently not satisfied with the effectiveness of our fire, although from our positions it appeared to be as good as it could get. Major Dennison called me on the radio and told me that closer fire support was needed, and asked if I could see a covered route to take a gun forward. I replied that there was no cover but I could get forward, and he replied with 'that will do'. I took the gun team from the high rocks on which they were positioned, and led them forward across the southern slope of the ridge. There was no clear advantage to be gained by moving forward, since the accuracy or the effect of the machine-gun's fire would not be improved by moving, and so it was not worth the risk. I did not question the order, however. There is no time for argument or debate when in close contact with the enemy. We were trained to obey battle orders instantly since to do otherwise would cause delays that might bring additions to the casualty list. I was proud to command men who would instantly respond to any orders I gave them, no matter how dangerous; in fact I found that my men seemed, when under fire, to be grateful to be told what to do and waited expectantly for the next order.

Moving carefully over what had been the scene of 1 Section, 6 Platoon's initial advance, after about a hundred metres I found a large slab of rock which offered some cover on this relatively open and gently sloping side of the ridge, and directed the SF crew to set up behind it. The tripod was levelled and the gun mounted and locked in position before additional ammunition was clipped on to the belt hanging from its left side. I indicated by radio that we were ready to fire, and when, after a frustrating delay and repeated requests from me, I was given the order I passed it to the Number One who began firing in bursts. Every fifth round in a belt was tracer, and bursts of twenty rounds or so were fired with pauses in between; therefore in each burst four or five red lines of tracer could be seen hitting the target area. Subsequent claims that all guns except one jammed and could not fire are nonsense – several thousand rounds were fired in a constant stream from all five guns in succession. Only one gun at a time was ordered to open fire, rather than all guns at once, which would have been more effective. Our fire poured on to Full Back, together with artillery, mortar and naval gunfire. I could not help thinking that B Company's attack ought to have been similarly supported.

Just before we were ordered to cease firing as A Company approached and assaulted Full Back, the enemy anti-tank gun near it was fired for the last time. I watched the flash of the gun and then the round streaked over my head before crashing into the rocks where I had left Stretch and the other two members of his Milan team.

A Company had advanced in a slow, methodical manner, moving one section at a time, clearing enemy positions with grenades as they went. The two forward platoons had been ordered to leave their webbing behind before advancing with just their weapons and ammunition. 1 Platoon had been forward left, 2 Platoon forward right and 3 Platoon to the rear in reserve. Major Collet's Company suffered only one minor casualty during the capture of Full Back – a man had been hit by a fragment from a 'friendly' grenade. The success of the attack was due to good leadership and the maximum use of firepower, as well as the skill of the attacking troops. I also believe that, at that late stage of the battle, the enemy had had enough, and many of the Argentine defenders were already retreating eastwards.

With A Company firmly in control of Full Back, I was called back to rejoin the rest of Support Company. My first concern was Stretch's Milan crew, as I assumed that one or more of them had been killed or injured by the anti-tank round. When I arrived at their position they were nowhere to be seen and I feared the worst, but I found them looking for loot in one of the Argentine tents, totally unscathed – the 105mm round had exploded close to them but on the other side of a small rock, which had shielded them from the blast. I felt like the parent of errant children who had strayed against instructions – angry yet at the same time full of relief that they were alive and well. When I returned to the Company HQ area I found Corporal Jim Morham, one of the Anti-tank Platoon men attached to 6 Platoon, with Ginge McCarthy dying in his arms. A shell had landed next to Ginge's Milan team. Others lay dead or dying. Mount Longdon was finally in our control after a battle lasting over nine hours. We had lost 19 men killed and over forty wounded. But the gods of war were not quite finished with us.

10. AFTERMATH

Death, of course, like chastity, admits of no degree; a man is either dead or not dead, and a man is just as dead by one means as by another; but it is infinitely more horrible and revolting to see a man shattered and eviscerated, than to see him shot. And one sees such things; and one suffers vicariously, with the inalienable sympathy of man for man. One forgets quickly. The mind is averted as well as the eyes ... And one moves on, leaving the mauled and bloody thing behind: gambling, in fact, on that implicit assurance each one of us has of his own immortality. One forgets, but he will remember again later, if only in sleep.

Frederick Manning, *The Middle Parts of Fortune*

The sky slowly grew paler and a thin mist enveloped the ridge. The enemy had made use of artillery and mortar fire during the battle, directed mainly at Fly Half, but now that it was clear to the Argentines that Mount Longdon was lost to them, they began to adjust their fire on to the whole of the ridge with a vengeance. As a hail of shells fell around the Support Company positions on Fly Half I ran over the frost-covered rocks through the blast waves and flying shrapnel, and jumped into a gap between two large rocks, letting out a whoop of joy as I landed unharmed. One of the men sheltering in the rocks looked askance at my odd behaviour – I must have appeared to be enjoying myself – and perhaps I was. Adrenalin had a part to play I am sure; it seemed that the closer I came to death the more intensely alive I felt.

It was time to consolidate our victory and reorganise. Dealing with casualties was a priority – some of the B Company wounded had been on the ridge in exposed positions for several hours and had not received any treatment. They were now carried from the hill through the bombardment to the Regimental Aid Post. Two men carrying a young private paused near me to rest and seek temporary shelter. I went over to look at the injured man, who had been shot through the ankle. The wound had not been dressed so I cut away his boot and strapped a large dressing around his ankle, covering the holes where the bullet had passed through – severing his Achilles tendon. His eyes and his nervous movements told me how frightened he was of the shells that continued to fall around us; I did my best to pretend that we were not in much danger and told him the standard reassuring lie that he would soon be on his feet and running about. Chris and Ollie were sheltering in a nearby sangar and had just made a brew of tea, which they shared with the wounded man. Chris had found an Argentine sleeping bag that he was rather pleased with until I persuaded him to give it to our wounded man, and we slid him into it before handing him over to the two men who took him down the hill towards the RAP. If they made it through the bombardment there was a chance that he would be evacuated by helicopter to the Field Dressing Station back at Teal Inlet.

The bodies of Ginge and one of his Milan crew lay behind us, covered with Argentine blankets and marked by their rifles stuck into the earth with their helmets on top. They had died when a shell exploded next to them as they waited for orders to deploy their firing post, which lay mangled beside them. Major Dennison called out for a casualty report. Apart from the two dead men all the Milan Section apart from the third man from Ginge's crew could be accounted for – I assumed that he was one of the men helping to carry wounded to the RAP. The OC was keen to move forward from Fly Half, which seemed to act as a magnet for shells, and he decided not to wait for the missing man.

We advanced in single file through the area that B Company had fought over in the darkness, the full savagery of the night battle now evident in the cold daylight. I felt as though I were walking through a surreal nightmare landscape or a waxworks 'chamber of horrors'. Here a grinning face on a pile of scorched flesh and clothing, there a blood-drenched corpse with half a head. All my 12 years of training, all the war films I had ever seen and all the military history books I had read had not been enough to prepare me for this, and my mind quickly closed the door to emotion in preparation for whatever grotesque tableau might be waiting around the next rock. Soldiers quickly develop the necessary immunity to the varied sights of death, and this creates an outward appearance of indifference and callousness. To dwell too much on the tragedy of it all would have the effect of weakening one's resolve – precisely what we were trying to do to the enemy. We just had to carry on being as efficient as possible, to keep the pressure on the Argentines until they cracked.

We moved forward along the ridge and down into the bowl and took up new positions in sangars built by the Argentines, where we began to brew tea and eat chocolate as if breakfasting on a hill covered in unburied corpses was something we did every day.

The enemy bombardment of Mount Longdon continued; there was to be little respite from shells for the next two days. We occupied positions that were on the northern side of the ridge and so for the most part we were out of sight of the enemy in Stanley and on Mount Tumbledown across the valley to our south. I chose a sangar on the northern rim of the bowl, and shared it with Chris and Ollie – it was just large enough to accommodate the three of us lying down, although whoever got in last had to lie near the exposed doorway. The walls were constructed of rocks and had wood and metal spanning them to support a roof of flat rocks, giving good protection from surrounding shellfire but a direct hit would probably have destroyed it. Our shelter was typical of the many sangars on the hill, constructed over the preceding two months and blending well into the natural rock walls that protruded from the earth.

The defenders of Mount Longdon had been men of B Company of the Argentine 7th Infantry Regiment, known as RI 7, who had arrived on East Falkland on 13 April and moved to Longdon the following day, five days after *Canberra* sailed from Southampton. The private soldiers of RI 7 were conscripted men from Buenos Aires who had recently completed one year of training. The conscripts were led by a cadre of regular officers and NCOs, and were reinforced by a Marine Heavy Machine-Gun (12.7mm) company, some engineers, anti-tank crews (of both recoilless rifles and guided missiles), and mortar (81mm and 120mm) crews. In terms of training and experience, when compared to the men of B Company 3 Para, for example, their opponents during the initial assault, the Argentines were the weaker side. In their favour had been the fact that they had been defending, which for the private soldier at least does not require as

178

much training and experience as other operations – put simply, a defending soldier only needs to fire his weapon from his protective defences at his attacker. The defender, as in this case, will usually hold the ground that makes life as difficult as possible for the attacking force – often this will be the dominant high ground, which means that most attacks are an uphill struggle. Another factor in favour of the defenders was the firepower available to them; from their automatic rifles to medium and heavy machine-guns, mortars and anti-tank guns. They also had an abundance of ammunition. There is also good evidence that Argentine Special Forces had bolstered the defence: the battle map used by General Menendez, which was found in Government House in Stanley after the surrender, indicated a Special Forces unit on Longdon in addition to RI 7, and Argentine prisoners also substantiated that fact.

The rocky nature of Mount Longdon made it easy in the ample time available to the enemy to turn the ridge into a fortress, although with more thought and effort it could have been made almost impregnable – some of the enemy positions were not well sited or as well constructed as they could have been – possibly they were built by late-arriving reinforcements. RI 7 had not used any barbed wire, sandbags or any of the usual 'defence stores' that we would certainly have employed. They had laid minefields around the hill, but if they had done it properly we would have suffered more mine casualties. They had not patrolled forward of their position effectively – or perhaps they had not patrolled at all – the large enemy patrol encountered by D Company was believed to be a Special Forces unit. The defenders lacked discipline in their defensive routine – sentries were either badly sited or asleep – they certainly were not using their radar and their numerous night-vision devices during our approach. For all that the Argentines had fought well enough to hold on to Mount Longdon for nine hours against an aggressive assault by superior troops; apart from their advantages of protective emplacements and the natural rock walls of the hill, how had they achieved this?

I believe that the main reason that our attack took so long and cost us so many casualties was the attempt to use surprise instead of firepower. Maximum use of naval gunfire, artillery and mortars before the initial assault, followed by a slowly creeping barrage along

179

the ridge during the subsequent fighting would have made far more sense. Once fire was exchanged and surprise lost, B Company were outgunned by the superior firepower of the enemy small arms, with their advancing men channelled by the terrain into open areas covered by fire from protected and concealed positions. In British Army teaching, both the element of surprise and the maximum use of firepower are considered to be ideal requirements for an attacking force, and a preliminary bombardment would not necessarily have led the enemy to believe that an attack was imminent. If the Commanding Officer had asked his Battalion for a show of hands (not that he should have done, of course) in favour of a preliminary bombardment of the objective as opposed to a silent approach, I am certain that everyone would have raise a hand without hesitation.

Ironically, the repeated success of our D Company recce patrols during their skilful forays on to Mount Longdon may have led our superiors to a false belief that a preliminary bombardment would not be necessary, and that once contact was made with our disorganised and demoralised enemy he would disintegrate before us. If the patrols had been unsuccessful then the 'silent attack' would probably not have been considered.

Even without a preliminary bombardment our fire teams of Milan and SF machine-guns could have been of much more use if we had been positioned to the north of the ridge and able to engage the enemy depth positions as B Company advanced from right to left across our front.

The direction chosen for the assault, from one end of the ridge to the other, meant that our superior numbers could not be used to our advantage – only one Company had room to manoeuvre within the width of the ridge, plus our Milan and SF machine-guns also had to find room on the ridge to support the second stage of the attack. The direction of attack also meant that the enemy had the advantage of 'depth', and were able to engage B Company from positions further along the ridge, even when they had successfully captured Fly Half.

There was an option of attacking from the north, which would have allowed two Companies room to attack side by side and hit every part of the enemy at once, but the disadvantage of that was that the enemy defences had been planned to counter an attack from the north.

A Battalion attack from the south, sweeping across the ridge from the Estancia–Stanley road on a two-company front, would have taken the Longdon defences in the rear. Such a daring move – advancing between Mount Longdon and Mount Tumbledown before turning to the north – could have become messy if the advance was discovered before the attack began, but given the fact that the enemy were not alert, could have worked. This option was probably ruled out because a minefield was thought to exist on the south side of the ridge, although it was unclear to me on what intelligence this was based. In fact there were unmarked minefields all around the western half of the hill, extending to the north and south. The whole of 3 Para moved through the minefields and suffered only one mine casualty. The men of 1 Section, 6 Platoon had made their initial advance along the southern slope unmolested – only when they moved on to the top of the ridge did they come under enemy fire, and after that time no further attempt was made to advance along the southern slopes – instead the whole of B Company became crowded into the rocky northern side of the ridge.

It was accepted practice in a company attack to advance either with two platoons forward and one in reserve, or one platoon forward and two in reserve. The OC of B Company had advanced his three platoons alongside each other, which was an unorthodox formation to say the least. The result was that all three platoons were under enemy fire at the same time, and there was no dedicated reserve. I assume that there was a good reason to depart from the standard methods, although I have failed to work out what it might have been.

An attack at night along the length of Mount Longdon was always going to be difficult to control, but the best area to attempt to do it from was the high ground along the centre of the ridge. Instead, B Company Headquarters followed 5 Platoon into the labyrinth of rocks on the northern slope.

The natural animal instincts of 'Freeze, Flight or Fight' when faced with extreme danger, were at work within our opponents during the attack. Some became paralysed and hid, hoping that the danger would pass them by; some chose to run away towards Moody Brook and Stanley; some fired their weapons hoping to put an end to the threat. Some might have done all three at different stages but enough of them chose to fight, turning the battle into an unexpectedly fierce contest. The Argentine officers on Longdon had told their soldiers cautionary tales about what English soldiers would do to them if they surrendered, which had probably been a good incentive to fight harder.

Could 3 Para have used a different plan to capture Mount Longdon and suffered fewer casualties? Probably – but not necessarily. It is easy for those of us who were not in command to criticise, and the criticism would have more justification if we had been defeated, but the battle was a victory, our mission was achieved, our enemies had either been killed, taken prisoner or fled, and we held Mount Longdon – the shell of the Port Stanley defences was broken.

———— •◆• ————

After my breakfast of tea and chocolate I went for a look around the hollow in search of a sleeping bag or any other useful items. Others wisely remained under cover or began to construct their own shelters but a few scavengers like myself wandered around the area. On my circuit of 'the bowl' I was surprised to see an Argentine soldier stagger through the rocks towards me, unarmed and unescorted. Three of us aimed our weapons at him as he rolled from side to side as if drunk, blood trickling down his face from beneath his helmet. His glazed eyes appeared not to notice us, and he toppled sideways with his left shoulder against a wall of rock as his legs buckled beneath him and he sank slowly to the ground as life drained from him. I took his photograph, as though I expected an image of the Spectre of Death to appear on the developed film instead of something that looked like a drunken soldier against a rock. It came as a surprise to me when I discovered long after the battle that the same man had actually survived, was taken prisoner and eventually returned to Argentina – a remarkable resurrection that would not have been possible if I had shot him, as I would have done in training, 'to make sure' (he was not surrendering). Whether he deliberately 'played possum' or not, we were certainly fooled. I cannot think why I did not shoot him but if he is alive, as I believe him to be, then good luck to him – his survival made no difference to our operations.

I do not know why, I suppose it was because I was used to the aftermath of the relatively neat training battles I had 'fought' in, but I was surprised by how *untidy* the battlefield was. The ridge was strewn with the litter of war. Clothing, ammunition, food, weapons, radios, batteries, boxes, bandages, boots and paper covered the area. The dead bodies of both sides looked unreal to the extent that they would not have been used in a war film because they looked 'unrealistic'– like poorly made wax dummies. I passed half of what looked like a face stuck to the side of a large rock, like a controversial Turner Prize exhibit.

Chris, another inveterate scavenger, returned with me to the area of our Milan and machine-gun fire positions of the night before. We inspected the unfired Cobra anti-tank missiles that were set up on the western slope of the hill, then I returned to the sangar I had crawled into and searched during the night, and ripped the telescopic sight of the control unit from its mounting, intending to keep it for my own use. My second search of the sangar uncovered the long, octagonal barrel of an Argentine signal pistol, designed to fire coloured flares into the air; engraved on the side of the barrel were the words, *'Ejercito Argentino'* – I put it in my loot bag, but continued to hope that I would find a .45 inch pistol.

Several times during our wanderings we were forced to take cover as shells landed around us, but we were becoming familiar with the different sounds of the approaching shells and could tell when it was reasonably safe to remain exposed. One salvo in particular, though, caught us in an open area with little cover and we had to flatten ourselves against the earth and hope for the best – the shells exploded all around us leaving us unharmed.

Chris inspected the mess beneath the blankets where the two Milan men had died and found a fifth leg – the third member of Ginge's crew had not gone to help with the wounded, after all. Stretcher-bearers were moving some of our dead back down to the northwest side of the hill, where the remains of B Company and the RAP were. According to the bearers who returned, the Padre there was overcome with grief. One of our men had carried a child's furry toy animal inside his smock as a good luck charm – it was carried away with his body. I soon found that I was able to look at the bodies of our men and feel absolutely no emotion at all, as if that part of my brain normally responsible for such feelings had been injected with anaesthetic. In fact I believe that we were all, to a greater or lesser extent, suffering from a kind of shock that inhibited our normal mental functioning.

The Commanding Officer moved past me along the edge of the bowl, looking sad yet determined, accompanied by the RSM and two radio operators. 'Sergeant Colbeck – I'm sorry to hear about Corporal McCarthy and his men – very sorry indeed,' he said. I could not think of an appropriate reply – I think I just said, 'Sir.'

The last phase of any attack, which we all knew very well, was 'Reorganisation'; it involved a search of the captured position, a rapid positioning of men and weapons to defend against counter-attack, redistribution of ammunition, casualty procedures and so on. This had not taken place in the Support Company area of the ridge with anything like the thoroughness it should have, mainly because of the continuous enemy shelling of our positions, but partly because nobody in command 'got a grip' of it. The area we occupied had been captured by B Company, the remnants of which had been withdrawn from the area before daylight. A systematic search of the hill should have taken place as soon as possible after first light, because after two or three hours of daylight we discovered live enemy soldiers in our area, some within a few yards of the positions we now occupied. I shared the responsibility for the oversight, which could have resulted in casualties if the hidden men been more tenacious, but instead they slowly emerged or were dragged from their hiding places in a tremulous state. I called for some more men to help and we had soon assembled a line of about ten prisoners, all of whom had been hiding in the area of the bowl. Most of the men were young (as were most of 3 Para) and two of them had shit themselves in terror. One had a leg wound that had been bandaged – it was later rumoured that the Argentine soldiers with leg wounds had been shot by their own officers to prevent them from running away. The line of pathetic, demoralised and bewildered boys had not, from their pitiful appearance, formed the backbone of the Argentine defence. They had been sent to fight for an emotive cause that they had quickly realised was not worth their lives. After searching them we gave them water and allowed them to clutch their rosary beads before they were led away to join the other prisoners taken during the night.

Some of the prisoners were later put to work on the northern side of the ridge burying the Argentine dead. This became the scene of the alleged 'war crime' incident described in the book, *Excursion to Hell* by Vincent Bramley and as a result investigated by the Metropolitan

Police. Although it was decided not to prosecute, there were several witnesses to the shooting dead of an Argentine prisoner of war by an A Company soldier. I do not condone the act but I do not find it surprising that it took place; if anything I am surprised that so many Argentines were taken prisoner – about fifty in total, many during the darkness and confusion of the night, and at some risk to the captors. Had I been there I would have tried to prevent the shooting, but I doubt if I would have taken any disciplinary action if I had been too late. I understood that when men live so near to the edge of life their minds can lose the ability to focus on the dividing lines between aggression and ruthlessness, and between ruthlessness and barbarity. The dividing lines may also have been blurred by the story of the white flag incident at Goose Green – no excuse, but revenge may have played a part. As to punishment of the perpetrator – in this case the realisation of what he did may be punishment enough, maybe not. I could have shot the wounded enemy soldier that 'died' in front of me; I did not and he survived – perhaps there was a kind of balancing effect at work there – Good balancing Evil. Battle is a delicate balance between extremes of human behaviour – selfish cowardice and selfless sacrifice, brutality and humanity, callousness and pity – and the virtuous must be made to outweigh the dishonourable, both in the individual and the unit, if either is to survive with any pride.

Any surrender is a gamble, and it would be a rather naïve soldier of a unit that has killed and wounded men over a ten-hour period who gives himself up to their friends expecting nothing but chivalrous treatment – yet that is what the vast majority received. Wars have always produced acts of unnecessary savagery; for the most part they are kept under control and not allowed to escalate into mass murder, torture and other acts that most men are capable of in extreme circumstances.

———— •◆• ————

Date: *Sat 12 June*
Place: *Mt Longdon*
Weather: *Fine day*
2120 hrs [5.20 p.m. local] *An eventful day . . . we await tomorrow's expected advance East towards Navy Point.*

185

The image of our first day on Mount Longdon that remains most vivid in my memory is that of the body of a young 3 Para 'Tom' – he had climbed up a gully between the enormous rocks on the north face of the ridge, emerging at the edge of the bowl in the middle of several enemy sangars, where he had been shot in the head. What compelled attention was the attitude in which the body was frozen: kneeling against a rock with head bowed, rifle with fixed bayonet pointing across the ridge, and an unpinned grenade clutched in his right hand. I briefly considered taking a photograph but it would have debased the memory of the living man. Chris put a pin in the grenade and unclipped a belt of machine-gun ammunition and removed it from around the body before it was taken away.

As dusk approached we could see the men of 2 Para advancing eastwards in the valley to our north, and we looked forward to a renewed push towards Stanley and some relief from the shelling. I broke up the expanded polystyrene packing of some Cobra missile cases and laid these on the floor of our sangar for insulation. When it grew dark I wrapped an Argentine blanket around me and slowly fell into a fitful sleep, my first in over thirty-six hours. The night was relatively quiet with little artillery fire in our direction until dawn of the following day, 13 June.

Artillery and mortar fire have unpredictable effects; a man can stand a couple of metres from the point of impact of a shell and remain unharmed – while shrapnel from the same explosion can kill a man 40 metres away. We developed our own theories about the trajectories of artillery and mortar projectiles, and tried to convince ourselves that the sangar we had chosen to shelter in offered the least chance of a direct hit. Some men claimed the ability to distinguish between the sounds of approaching artillery shells and mortar bombs, but I was never sure. Mortar bombs fall more steeply than artillery shells and are supposed to give less warning of their arrival. The theory went that mortar bombs were more likely to land on the steep northern slope where we sheltered than artillery shells, which would either under or overshoot. It made no difference to me whether the sky rained mortar bombs or artillery shells – they were equally deadly and usually accurate. With each approaching scream I convinced myself that the coming explosion would tear off a part of my body – sometimes an arm, sometimes my head – and each time the impact left me unharmed I felt reborn. I was like a player of Russian Roulette who hears with relief the click of his revolver's hammer on an empty chamber. It took great effort at times to remain calm under a rain of such terrible power, as with each crash the jagged shrapnel smacked into the rocks around me. I picked up one of the bright slivers of steel and found it too hot to hold.

During the time of the most concentrated bombardment of our position I asked myself if I would rather be safe back in England; oddly enough the answer was a sincere, 'No.' A shell exploded near Stretch; shrapnel penetrated his webbing and lodged in his camera. The same explosion sent fragments of steel into his Milan firing post – a tiny piece entered the sensitive tracking unit which appeared to remain serviceable but we had no way of checking for sure – our heavy electrical test unit had not been brought forward. Including Stretch's unit, there were now four Milan firing posts and crews left from the original six.

I spoke to some men from 2 Para after the final surrender who told me that they were amazed to see, from their position to the north, men wandering around Mount Longdon apparently oblivious of the shells that fell around them. Some men found it preferable to keep themselves occupied by collecting bits of enemy equipment than to sit in a sangar and wait for it to become their tomb. I had noticed that most men when under shellfire instinctively tended to spread their hands over their helmets; I decided that this was unwise and determined to resist the action – sometimes without success. The Argentine artillerymen at one stage used fuses that caused their shells to burst over our heads rather than on impact, but I believe that the airbursts had less effect – I watched (unwisely) as several shells burst in the sky above us. I had the unnerving experience during one bombardment of looking into the eyes of someone close by – it was as if I suddenly saw straight into his fear, and this was immediately infectious. I tended to avoid looking at eyes after that experience. The defenders of Port Stanley must have thought that they could dislodge us from Mount Longdon by the use of indirect fire alone, but the only way they could effectively defend at that stage would have been to counter-attack, which was something they could not achieve without the necessary leadership, determination and courage.

I would have welcomed the chance to defend Mount Longdon

against a counter-attack – then we would have seen how the Argentines looked as we slaughtered them in the open from our rocky fortress. An enemy attack, however, would probably have come from the east or south, and Support Company were not best placed to deal with it – we were sheltering on the northern, reverse slope and would have had to re-deploy to support A Company, who would have taken the brunt of the attack. Ammunition was plentiful – we each had more than we were likely to need with our captured stock of 7.62mm. We even had a choice of extra weapons so that we would save time reloading. Some men even carried an enemy rifle in preference to their own SLR, because of the automatic capability.

Most of us were now using some form of captured Argentine equipment; many had ditched their DMS boots and were wearing boots taken from dead enemy soldiers. The Argentine ration boxes we ate from contained small blue matchboxes, each with a picture of a warship on the front. I began to collect them, and swapped them with other collectors to build up a set – like schoolboys collecting picture cards from bubblegum packets – 'Swap you a *General Belgrano* for a *25th May*?' My bag of loot was growing heavier, and I replaced my sandbag with one of the large enemy ammunition pouches, which had a shoulder-strap, and transferred my assorted collection to it.

After searching sangars on the southern slope of the ridge, Chris and I each possessed a pistol. Chris had a .45 inch and I carried a 9mm pistol, taken from a holster on one of three Argentine bodies in a roofless sangar, together with extra magazines of ammunition. Many of the enemy dead had been taken off the hill by our prisoners and buried in shallow graves, but there were still many more remaining unburied where they had died, particularly in places that were exposed to the south and Mount Tumbledown – still in enemy hands, which was disappointing to us as we had expected it to be attacked during the night – it was one of the objectives of 5 Infantry Brigade.

Sitting on top of the Mount Longdon ridge and facing south across the valley to Mount Tumbledown was one of the abandoned enemy 105mm recoilless anti-tank guns, similar to our Wombats left behind on *Canberra*. Chris and I decided to fire it towards Tumbledown, more in a defiant gesture than with any hope of doing any real damage at that range (about two kilometres). As we were trying to work out how to operate the firing mechanism, I saw a head beneath an Argentine helmet appear above a rock about fifty metres down the slope – the enemy soldier dropped out of sight as I brought my rifle into the aim. Chris and I both took cover behind the low rock walls of the gun emplacement and waited for him to reappear, our sights aligned at the spot where he had disappeared; it would have been an easy shot. A few seconds later two arms were raised above the rock in surrender, followed by a head. We moved down the slope to take the man prisoner. Spread-eagled with his hands against the rock as Chris searched him, he gave me a nervous smile when he realised that we were not sub-human after all. He had been sheltering in a hollow below a large slab of rock, not far from where I had positioned the SF machine-gun when I was sent forward on the night of our attack. The southern slope where we had found the soldier had not been searched because of its exposure to Mount Tumbledown. We took the man back over the top of the ridge to join the other prisoners.

Chris found two of our B Company dead on top of the ridge, and we sent for stretcher-bearers. The corpses lay alongside each other. One of them appeared to have died in agony – he lay on his back with his lower arms and clenched fists thrust into the air. Parted lips revealed clenched teeth, and his open eyes had accused the stars. We lifted the body on to a stretcher and it was carried off the ridge. The arms would have to be broken to fit inside a 'Bag – Human Remains'. I had been annoyed to find two of our dead still in position on the second day, which is illogical, since it made absolutely no difference if they had been removed 24 hours earlier or two weeks later. It also defies logic to see stretcher-bearers (so-called 'REMFs') carrying a corpse while shells exploded around them, as if they were carrying the man to safety – but it happened.

Private Harley called to us from the top of the ridge – he had found a severed arm that belonged to one of our dead bodies and was taking it to the Padre. In retrospect this act seems pointless, even macabre – but at the time it had meaning. A similar reverence for our dead seems to have prevented any photography of them, whereas the vanquished enemy were regarded as a much lower form of death.

Tom Smith, the press photographer, came up to our position and I hung my Union Jack over the side of our sangar before he took a photograph of us. I decided to leave the flag in position and I went with Chris to explore another part of the ridge further to the east towards A Company. We followed one of the Milan control wires and discovered that the missile had flown above an enemy sniper position – a pile of empty bullet cases lay there. The sniper had chosen a perfect place from which to fire on B Company – a natural gap in the rocks formed by a fallen slab that gave excellent protection and a covered escape route. Of course it had been impossible to tell if we had been fired on by an actual sniper during the battle – any rifleman can 'snipe' but only a select few are properly trained and equipped to do so. However, Corporal Mick Mathews, one of the Milan detachment commanders, showed me a night 'scope that he had taken from a captured sniper rifle. It was half the size and weight of British image-intensifiers; the green image it produced had a red aiming dot in the centre.

On top of the ridge near A Company's area sat a 12.7mm heavy machine-gun, one of many that had caused us problems during the battle. The gun became our next project. A Naval Gunfire Observer, Captain Willie McCracken, had settled himself behind some nearby rocks and was busy directing fire on to enemy positions around Port Stanley. When he saw Chris and me playing with the gun he asked, 'You're not going to fire that thing are you?' He was smiling so we assumed that he was not that concerned, and we continued to prepare the gun for firing. Neither of us had fired that particular type of machine-gun before and we knew very little about it, but Chris was soon firing long bursts that flew in a high arc in the direction of Sapper Hill, over five kilometres away – beyond the effective maximum range of the gun but it looked and sounded good. After several long bursts the gun jammed with a round stuck in the breech, and while Chris tried to extract it I searched a pile of enemy equipment and found some letters, one of which contained a long list of football results.

There were also letters from children addressed, 'PARA UN CONSCRIPTO' – to a conscript. Just as schoolchildren back in England had written in a similar way to the Task Force, addressing letters to the *Canberra*. The eternal irony of course is that the same children from both countries would probably play quite happily with each other in the same schoolyard.

The machine-gun seemed permanently jammed unless we could

replace the barrel with one from another gun, so we decided to fetch one from a gun near the Support Company position. Before we left a salvo of artillery fire fell around us – it was the enemy's way of saying, 'Don't fire that gun again!' We assumed that the Argentine artillery fire was being controlled by an observer on Mount Tumbledown. I felt that something ought to have been done about the Argentine artillery – if it was impossible to bring our own artillery within range of theirs, then why were the enemy guns not bombed from the air, or shelled from our ships? Perhaps it was because the enemy guns were positioned close to Stanley, but it should have been possible to put the majority of them out of action with minimum risk to civilians.

On the way to collect another barrel I spotted a bloodstained wristwatch on the ground and slipped it into my pocket. We saw two Royal Artillery men from a Blowpipe Detachment wearing Argentine helmets in preference to their own, non-Airborne issue 'tin hats'– but without regard to the fact that they could be mistakenly shot by our troops as a result. We advised the men to take the helmets off. On reaching the other 12.7mm we detached the barrel and collected two belts of ammunition before returning to the jammed gun. Captain McCracken observed our return with a look of fake dismay, but the repaired gun only fired a few more bursts before jamming again. On returning to our sangar we found that Ollie, concerned that it would attract fire, had wisely taken my Union Jack inside.

Major Dennison told us that 2 Para would attack Wireless Ridge that night and our Support Company fire teams would add fire support from the eastern slope of Mount Longdon, so Chris and I went forward to look for fire positions, taking Phil, our sniper, with us. On the way we stopped to inspect A Company's haul of enemy weapons and equipment, which included a Soviet surface-to-air missile, shoulder-fired (NATO codename *Grail*), and a French radar. As we passed through A Company's position one of the men from Patrol Company who was manning an observation post on the southwest side of the ridge, warned us to take cover because they were under fire from Tumbledown Mountain and the valley below. We left Phil there in the hope that he could be of some use with his sniper rifle, and ran down the eastern slope of Mount Longdon to a spot that gave us a good view of Wireless Ridge.

I scanned the area to the east and marked the main enemy locations on my map. It was clear that the Argentines occupied not just Wireless Ridge itself but areas of high ground to the north of it. I could easily see individual trenches and sangars, and at times spotted soldiers moving around. To get the enemy within effective range of our SF machine-guns it would be necessary to move some distance down the eastern slope of Longdon towards Wireless Ridge. From where we lay we could clearly see Port Stanley and the enemy artillery batteries near the Racecourse that were firing at us. Chris thought that he could also see a camouflaged Islander aircraft on the Racecourse. We debated the wisdom of returning to a position closer to Wireless Ridge with a Milan firing post and a couple of missiles, and having a go at an enemy bunker, but eventually decided against it. It turned out to be a good decision for a reason we were not aware of at the time – the firing post I would have used was later found to be useless because of the shrapnel in it. We retraced our steps and collected our sniper, who we found drinking tea in a sangar; we were annoyed to find that he had not fired a single shot. On our way back to the bowl we visited Captain McCracken and Chris gave him the map reference of the Islander aircraft in the hope that he could get his guns to fire at it.

On our way back we met Colonel Chaundler, the replacement Commanding Officer for the dead Colonel Jones of 2 Para. The new CO was going forward along Mount Longdon to look at enemy dispositions on Wireless Ridge in preparation for 2 Para's attack planned for that night. I showed him the enemy locations I had marked on my map. He mentioned that our C Company had not moved as far forward on the north side of Longdon as they were supposed to have, and we agreed. Before he moved on he also said that he would appreciate as much fire support as possible for the attack.

I had very little water left by now; there had been no rain since we left Estancia – only a couple of light flurries of snow in the night, and on Mount Longdon there were no streams within easy reach – so I walked down the slope to the north, towards the low ground where 2 Para were preparing for their attack on Wireless Ridge. I could only find some brackish water in the bottom of a shell crater and so I filled a bottle with that – it made the worst tea I have ever tasted.

In the late afternoon the Platoon Commander's signaller, Denzil

Connick, after hearing a rumour that a resupply including cigarettes had been delivered by one of the casevac helicopters to the western side of Mount Longdon, decided to go and investigate. On his way along the northern edge of the ridge he was severely wounded when an artillery shell exploded between him and two other men, taking off his left leg and damaging his right. The two other men, both REME technicians who had been acting as stretcher-bearers, were killed. I visited Denzil several weeks later in Woolwich Military Hospital, where he remarked 'People always told me that smoking could damage my health.'

Snow began to fall as it grew dark and we were briefed by the OC for our role in 2 Para's attack. Our fire teams would remain the same as for the Mount Longdon attack, except of course for one Milan crew who were all dead. Our Mortars would also add their fire to that of 2 Para's Mortar Platoon. So, with my Milan and SF machine-gun crews behind me in single file I set off at the tail of the Support Company column that meandered eastwards along the ridge, through A Company's position and down past the spot where Chris and I had observed the enemy from during the afternoon. I was to take up fire positions behind and above the other two fire teams. As we approached our intended positions, I received a whispered message on my radio – someone had spotted a patrol approaching his location. I deployed the machine-gun in anticipation of a firefight, but the 'patrol' was discovered to be Captain Mason's fire team. The Anti-tank Platoon Commander had by this time earned himself the nickname, 'Bimbler', awarded to him by Major Dennison because of his misguided wanderings. I moved forward to my allotted position and indicated where the crews were to set up their weapons facing Wireless Ridge and pointing over the heads of the other fire teams on the slopes below.

As we waited for 2 Para's attack to start we were shelled again – our exposed positions on the forward slope had obviously attracted the attention of the Argentines on Wireless Ridge or Mount Tumbledown. The enemy were understandably more alert now than they had been prior to our attack on Mount Longdon, and must have been using their image-intensifiers or radar. The shelling was heavy and concentrated on my team's location. Fortunately we had set up in an area less rocky than most, and the shells lost some of their effectiveness in the soft earth, but there was little cover so I ordered the crews to leave their support weapons in place and seek cover in a group of overhanging rocks to our right. When the shellfire appeared to have ceased, Shakespeare called me by radio and asked if we were OK. There was laughter from Stretch's Milan crew – the seclusion afforded by the rocks we sheltered in had also recommended the spot to the Argies as a toilet – Stretch had been unlucky in his choice of cover and had thrown himself into the heart of the latrine.

The bombardment of Wireless Ridge and the features to the north of it began shortly after 9 p.m. My machine-gunner and Stretch with his Milan were poised with their safety catches off, awaiting the order to fire. Naval gunfire, artillery and mortar fire gave an impressive display, made more dramatic by the addition of flares that spiralled downwards on parachutes over the enemy defences. Tracer fire from 2 Para's machine-guns and those of the Blues and Royals, together with their cannon, hammered into the hillside, supplemented by the trail of Milan missiles – but our weapons sat silently in position. The OC did not give the order to open fire. Once again there was a reluctance to use our SF machine-guns and Milan, as if to do so would invite unwelcome retaliation; perhaps it would, but such is war. 2 Para fired over twenty Milan missiles during the Campaign, 3 Para fired five – one of the five had a flight malfunction and another was fired at a jet fighter; only three missiles flew to their targets on Mount Longdon.

All we could do was watch as 2 Para swept across and overwhelmed the enemy positions on Wireless Ridge. When the battle was won we pulled out of our fire positions and moved back up towards the bowl on Mount Longdon, feeling disappointed. Perhaps we had made a small contribution by distracting the Argentine artillery for a while. I led the way back over the snow-covered ridge, pausing only when challenged by an A Company sentry, and returned to my lair in the rocks.

11. VICTORY

The sun of our shield that justice illumines
Has cast out the shadows of that bitter darkness
And people of the world today are shouting,
'Argentina!'
> Translation of the last verse of a poem in Spanish found by
> the author in Port Stanley

———— •◆• ————

After the bleak dawn of 14 June, I waited to be briefed for an attack by 3 Para on Moody Brook Barracks and Stanley Racecourse. A thin carpet of snow covered Mount Longdon and there was an unusual silence – we had not been shelled since the attack on Wireless Ridge – the attention of the enemy had shifted in the night to 2 Para, who were now the closest unit to Stanley and the greater threat. I abandoned some of the heavier items in my collection of loot, including half a dozen bayonets, in preparation for the long-overdue move forward and the forthcoming attack.

There was a sudden commotion as shouted orders were relayed around our positions on the hill – 'Prepare to move!' It appeared that the timing of our attack had been brought forward, but we were then told that 2 Para, detecting signs of a collapse in enemy resistance, had seized the opportunity to take our objective – Moody Brook. In fact 2 Para had gone beyond that and were pursuing the retreating Argentines towards Port Stanley. 3 Para were not going to be left out and we quickly abandoned Mount Longdon and advanced, with our A Company leading, towards Wireless Ridge and Stanley.

As I led my fire team out of the boggy low ground and up towards Wireless Ridge I received a radio message – 'The enemy are running away – take off your helmets and put your berets on.' I stopped and turned to my men to pass on the order before attaching my helmet to my webbing. I then took my crumpled beret out of my helmet and put it on, using the action to cover up the fact that I was wiping tears from my cheeks, and continued towards the rocks on top of Wireless Ridge.

A rifle stood with its muzzle stuck in the ground at the top of the ridge and marked the body of a 2 Para soldier. I noticed that he wore rubber NBC over-boots to keep his feet dry. The waterproof jacket that had been used to cover his face had been blown aside and was flapping in the wind; I walked over and replaced it (why did I feel the need to do that?). As I passed through the rocks and descended towards Moody Brook I could see long lines of red berets stretching ahead of me all the way to Port Stanley.

Milan missiles had been fired towards Moody Brook by 2 Para and the missile control wires lay along the ground between there and Wireless Ridge. A poorly camouflaged Huey helicopter sat near the track that led eastwards towards the town. A Bandwagon came up the track behind us and we put the Milan firing posts and missiles on it as well as the SF gun tripods. The Mortar Platoon from 2 Para tabbed past us and one of them smiled and said, 'Well done the other night, lads.' 'And yourselves,' was the reply.

The track to Stanley turned into a tarmac road and we walked up it past the burnt wreckage of the Islander aircraft that Chris had pointed out to the NGFO the previous day. To the right of the road was Stanley Racecourse and the deserted Argentine artillery position, with eighteen 105mm Pack Howitzers in gun emplacements, all pointing westwards and surrounded by empty shell cases. On the edge of the town to the left of the road we passed a large seaplane hangar painted with red crosses on white circles, followed on the right by a long row of bungalows. The staggered file formation we were using, with a well-spaced line of men on each side of the road, had become disorganised – we were too relaxed and bunched up, so I warned my men behind me to spread out and stay alert. I was determined, if this was the end, that we would not finish our long journey looking like a rabble with bad march discipline.

We were halted by the bungalows with orders not to go any further into the town, and we found shelter from the rain in a large hut in one of the rear gardens. A hen had laid three eggs on some straw in a corner of the hut, which were boiled and eaten as I made a brief entry in my diary:

Date: *14 June 1982, Monday*
Place: *Stanley*
Weather: *Snow, sleet, sun*
The enemy have surrendered.
  2 PARA attacked Wireless Ridge last night and pushed on to Moody Barracks this afternoon. The defence folded then and we quickly left Longdon and followed 2 PARA into the town.

I left the hut to find that a door to one of the bungalows had been forced and some of my men were inside. A bearded Falkland Islands policeman who had acted as a guide for Patrol Company was angrily trying to remove the men – 'Even the Argies didn't break into our homes!' He was wrong there, but I saw his point and ordered the men to leave the house. They protested that permission to occupy the bungalows had come from the CO, and the policeman stormed off to go and speak to him. We were in fact allowed to use the houses and each Company of the Battalion was allocated a number of houses to move into. I wanted to fly my Union Jack somewhere and found a long TV aerial mast at the back of a bungalow to tie it to. With the help of some others we raised the mast and lashed it to a post in a garden. Shortly afterwards an Argentine helicopter pilot, probably believing that the flag marked a headquarters, landed his Huey in the field at the back of the house and ceremoniously surrendered his pistol to Captain Mason.

We were warned to keep our weapons loaded in case there were still enemy around who had not learned of the surrender. The Argentine troops on West Falkland had not surrendered and we were told that we might have to fight for that as well. When I heard that I became angry at the thought of having to continue fighting – I felt that we had done enough. For the first time I felt that I could actually come to hate the Argentine soldiers, who until now I had regarded simply as opponents to be defeated in a contest for possession of territory. The Argentines were well and truly beaten and if any of them continued to prolong the war by resisting then I am sure that I would have become far more ruthless in my encounters with them than I had been so far. Looking back, I can see that if I had managed to hate the Argentines in the same way that I found it easy to hate the IRA, I may well have been a more effective soldier. Perhaps the most ruthlessly efficient infantryman is one who goes into battle in a berserk state of unstoppable rage. Such a man would, though, be more likely to commit atrocities.

Somebody back at Estancia House was looking after us – Sea Kings ferried our bergens forward and as each helicopter deposited its load they were laid out in long rows in front of the Racecourse grandstand, together with our sea kitbags containing our follow-up kit. After a long search I found my belongings and returned to one of the bungalows that had been allocated to the Anti-tank Platoon. I unrolled my sleeping bag on the bedroom floor, climbed inside and immediately fell asleep.

Not long afterwards I was woken to take my turn on stag at the Company HQ radio outside the bungalow. During my duty I received a radio message that was sent to all stations on the Battalion net, informing us that the Argentine forces on West Falkland had surrendered; I was relieved to hear it. When I woke my replacement for his duty at the radio I passed on the message; he refused to believe me, accusing me of trying to start a rumour.

In the morning I washed and shaved, and changed some of my dirty clothing for clean. I then went to look at the Argentine artillery near the Racecourse. I found a kitbag and began to fill it with souvenirs and other loot – brass 105mm cases, letters, a telescope, a pair of gloves. As I crawled into the abandoned sangars with my torch I was well aware that I could easily become the victim of a booby-trap, but the thought made no difference to me. I found a wooden officer's chest that contained a map of the area. The map had been printed after a survey in 1942 by British Royal Engineers but it had been overprinted in Spanish: 'FALKLAND ISLANDS' had 'ISLAS MALVINAS' printed in bold letters below it. The map showed more detail of the terrain than the ones that British troops had been issued with; for example, the prominent rocks on Mount Longdon were clearly shown. The chest also contained two white heavy woollen cardigans; I stuffed them into my kitbag. I was envious when Chris, who had just crawled out of a sangar higher up the hillside, told me that he had found some binoculars.

Back at the bungalow, I watched as the Royal Marines marched down the road past us and into Stanley. The two Para Battalions had been stopped short of the centre of town, the World War One memorial at the end of the row of bungalows was the designated limit of our advance, although some had gone further, reaching Government House. If the final battles for Stanley had gone according to plan, the Marines would have entered the town first, which would have been considered more appropriate, I am sure. Instead, the Union Jack that 2 Para had hoisted on the flagpole outside Government House had to be taken down and the Marines replaced it with the original one that had flown there before the Argentine invasion.

Date: 15 June 1982, Tuesday
Place: Stanley
Weather: Windy, rain, hail, cold
2115 hours: [5.15 p.m. local] *Now in a house which has been looted by the enemy. The owner has returned and he says that he left a few days ago when the shelling got rather close.*

Some of the enemy guns are behind the house and the gun position stretches for about half a mile to the west. At 0230 hours [10.30 p.m. 14 June local] *this morning I learned that the enemy have accepted unconditional surrender so it's all over. We thought we might have to take West Falkland as well.*

Gangs of prisoners were shepherded around and engaged in various cleaning-up tasks such as filling trenches and repairing damage. The Argentine officers had, at their request, been allowed to retain their pistols because they needed them to protect themselves against their men. The request speaks volumes about the style and quality of their leadership.

We remained in Port Stanley for 12 days and since there was little to do there was ample time for reflection. There was some discussion, of course, about our experiences on Mount Longdon. Many men were bitter about the method of our attack; in particular the initial lack of fire support. There were tales of extraordinary courage. As a single man I had held a theory that family men, having more to live for, would tend to be over-cautious, and therefore less effective in battle. I had even advocated, with tongue in cheek, the forming of a company of unmarried soldiers in the Battalion who would act as 'stormtroopers' in the van of any attack. In fact the Battle of Mount Longdon proved my theory to have been entirely wrong.

3 Para casualties during the battle and the subsequent shelling totalled seventy: 23 killed and 47 wounded. There were dozens of close shaves; some men had bullet strikes on their helmets, others pieces of shrapnel in their equipment. B Company plus its attached men, having fought the initial part of the battle, had borne the brunt of the casualties. With 3 Para's 70 battle casualties added to those wounded by friendly fire or immobilised by frost-bite and severe trench foot, after this short Campaign the Battalion was now effectively under-strength by the equivalent of one Company. Of the six Milan firing posts we had carried ashore, only three were still capable of firing a missile.

There were times during the days in Stanley when I felt guilty at having survived unscathed, and I tormented myself with thoughts that I had not done enough during the battle:

'Why, when you knew there were wounded lying in the open on top of the ridge, did you not go forward to help them?'
   'Because others had already tried and were killed.'
   'But you may have succeeded where they had failed.'
   'I couldn't see any wounded – I heard no calls for help.'
   'Does that mean that they were dead?'
   'No – but it wasn't my job to bring in wounded – I had a fire team to command.'
   'It was not your job to man a firing post, but you did. It was not your job to rescue wounded, but you could have. Were you afraid?'
   'No! – I was never afraid – and no one who saw me can say that I ever showed fear.'
   'In that case you have no excuse.'

The days of waiting passed in a relaxed routine of administration, scavenging for Argie souvenirs, eating the same old rations and rushing to the latrine in the field at the back of the bungalow. We all, eventually, became afflicted by a malfunctioning of the bowels that became known as 'Galtieri's Revenge'. Major Dennison claimed that it was because of a failure to clean our mess tins properly – so I had to smile when I saw him dashing in the direction of the latrine in the middle of the night. The latrine – an old enemy trench – was used because the town's sewerage system had failed due to over-use.

The officers busied themselves writing medal citations. I thought that someone should have congratulated the men on their recent efforts, and when it became clear that this was not going to happen I did it myself. There was a very well received telegram from Prince Charles, the Colonel-in-Chief of the Parachute Regiment, which had been sent after the Mount Longdon battle but before the Argentine surrender:

FROM: BUCKINGHAM PALACE
I HAVE JUST HEARD THE NEWS OF THE 3RD BATTALION'S GALLANT ACTION AND WANTED TO SEND YOU ALL MY DEEPEST SYMPATHY FOR THE LOSSES YOU HAVE SUS-TAINED AMONGST YOUR FRIENDS AND COLLEAGUES. I AM SURE YOU WILL NOT HAVE TIME FOR SUCH THINGS BUT MY VERY BEST WISHES GO TO ALL THOSE WHO WERE WOUNDED IN THE OPERATION. IT IS ONLY TOO CLEAR THAT DESPITE APPALLING CONDITIONS OF THE MOST TESTING KIND THE 3RD BATTALION HAS LIVED UP TO THE EXTRAORDINARY COURAGEOUS TRADITIONS OF THE PARACHUTE REGIMENT AND HAS GIVEN US ALL REASON TO BE INTENSELY PROUD OF WHAT YOU ARE DOING SO FAR FROM HOME. MY THOUGHTS AND PRAY-ERS ARE CONSTANTLY WITH YOU FOR WHATEVER YOU HAVE TO DO NEXT AND I CAN ONLY SAY THAT IT IS THE GREATEST PRIVILEGE TO BE ASSOCIATED WITH SUCH A MAGNIFICENT REGIMENT.
SIGNED: CHARLES
           COLONEL IN CHIEF

On the afternoon of 15 June, Corporal 'Taff' Richardson of the Wombat Platoon and I gave ourselves a mission: to 'capture' an Argentine anti-tank gun as a trophy for our Anti-tank Platoon. We had seen one in an emplacement near the road towards Moody Brook, it was the same type as the guns on Mount Longdon, and pointed north across the water of the port towards Wireless Ridge. After some difficulty we placed the gun in its travelling position on its wheels and manhandled it to the road, intending to pull it back to town, but a Royal Marine was heading that way in a Bandwagon and offered to tow it for us. In this way our prize ended up in the garden of our bungalow (number 26). Our Mortar Platoon had a similar idea, and acquired two Argentine mortars – one a giant 120mm and the other a French made (Hotchkiss-Brandt) of 81mm calibre, of similar design and the same calibre as the mortars used by 3 Para. An order was given to surrender all the pistols and other assorted weapons that had been collected by individuals in the Battalion; I had expected this, but I was annoyed that the order also included night-vision goggles and sights – I had planned to keep my captured goggles.

I ventured into the centre of town, passing Government House which showed no sign of the battle that was supposed to have raged around it; even its glass conservatory was intact. At the docks I was rewarded with my first sight of an ideal target for Milan missiles – a row of armoured cars – French-built with 90mm cannon as their main armament. I climbed inside one – it looked brand new, and the ammunition racks were full. Nearby was a warehouse full of Argentine stores and rations, but it was guarded by military police-men. I saw Graham Russell driving around in a commandeered Argie 'jeep', which provided an opportunity to take a sightseeing tour of Stanley Airfield, even though it had been placed out of bounds to us. At the edge of town we stopped to inspect four giant 155mm artillery pieces – they were not in fire positions but parked alongside buildings. These guns were an addition to the eighteen 105mm howitzers I had counted. Sat alongside the road to the airfield was an Exocet anti-ship missile container/launcher, with two missile units side-by-side – per-haps the same launcher responsible for sinking HMS *Glamorgan* during its shore bombardment in support of 45 Commando's attack on Two Sisters on 12 June. The Exocets would have made an ideal target for attack by Harriers or Special Forces.

Stanley Airfield itself had been protected by anti-aircraft missiles and cannon, including a German-built twin 30mm. As Graham drove up the runway, it became clear that it had survived the bombing raids by Vulcans and Harriers, and I took some photographs of wrecked enemy aircraft before we were chased away by an angry RAF officer.

Our lazy days in Stanley provided a fertile ground for the devel-opment of the Rumour Weed. The sad news that Denzil Connick had died on the hospital ship, *Uganda*, came as the RSM was chatting to us; he strode away to check the information and returned, annoyed but relieved, to counter the story – Denzil stood a good chance of survival. Another rumour described a collection of ears that was found in the webbing belonging to one of our dead men. If the rumour were true, and it would not surprise me, then the fact that the 3 Para soldier was dead may have been in some way a levelling of the balance. I collected matchboxes and bayonets, another collected ears, what had belonged to our enemies was now ours, it was simply the result of a blurring of the dividing line between what was acceptable and what was not. To the primitive man in us, an ear is just another trophy.

Yet another story circulated that mercenaries from the United States had been encountered among the defenders of Mount Long-don, and the rumour gained credence even though there appeared to be little or no evidence for it – possibly only the fact that some of the prisoners may have spoken English with an American accent.

On 17 June we switched our watches from 'Zulu' to the local time zone. The Battalion held a memorial service in the church in Stanley. It was a sunny day and we marched in three ranks down the road to the church. Of the actual service I remember little but the uneasy two minutes' silence for the dead – each man alone with his thoughts.

I arranged a seat for myself on a helicopter flight that was going to Teal Inlet to visit the place where some of our dead had been buried. The Sea King flew over the route of 3 Para's advance from Teal, and put down in the Settlement, which had been an important staging-post for 3 Commando Brigade. A row of simple wooden crosses marked the graves that had been dug on a slope not far above the water's edge. If there is such a thing as an ideal final resting place, I thought, then this tranquil spot must be it; when the litter of war had been cleared away the small community could revert to a peaceful existence and tend the graves of those who had liberated them. The bodies were later dug up and moved to San Carlos, and then some were shipped back to England at the request of relatives – setting, I believe, a precedent that may be regretted in future. British soldiers have traditionally been buried near the place they fell, or where they later died of wounds – why should this latest 'foreign field' have been any different?

As we passed Mount Longdon on the return flight, I moved forward to the cockpit of the Sea King so that I could take a photograph. From the air it was difficult to equate the peaceful, barren hill with the one that had been the scene of so much anguish.

Scavenging and general sightseeing became increasingly difficult as peacetime Army restrictions began to be imposed and the Royal Military Police found a role. Former enemy emplacements were declared out of bounds because of the booby-trap risk.

To fill the empty hours I tried to read books, but I found that I could 'read' whole chapters without registering a word, and after many attempts I gave up. For several days I lived in a sort of mental no man's land, feeling neither happy or sad, and unable to con- centrate on anything for long. Chris and Ollie had found a large Argentine tent and they erected it in the front garden of our bunga- low, so I moved in with them, glad to be out of the house where I had felt like an uninvited guest. While in the tent I was visited by an old friend from the Vigilant Platoon. Now with the SAS, his Squadron had arrived in the Falklands by parachuting into the sea, but they had been too late to play an active part in operations.

The *Canberra* and the *Norland* were used to carry prisoners back to Argentina. A story passed around by one of the 3 Para men acting as a prisoner guard told of an Argentine soldier who had tried to board the *Canberra* with the body of his brother in a kitbag.

A son was born to Prince Charles and Princess Diana on 21 June, and a telegram of congratulations was sent from the Parachute Bat- talions. In reply, our Colonel-in-Chief ended by saying that their son would not be called, 'Stanley'.

Arrangements were made for our return to England – we were to sail with 2 Para on the *Norland*, perhaps to keep us apart from the Marines. When the ship returned from Argentina and anchored in Port Stanley, we marched into town to queue for a ferry ride to the ship. As I climbed down from the quay on to a Mexefloat raft, two Royal Marines disembarked and started to walk into Stanley; one of the 3 Para men in the queue shouted out to them, 'Don't give it away again, will you?' The Marines smiled.

12. RETURN

You gallant sons of Britain, I pray you lend an ear,
Stir up your noble courage, boys, and enter volunteers;
We'll cross the raging seas, and fight for the King,
And, when we do return again, in claret we will swim.
                    'Light Horse', eighteenth-century English ballad

————— •◆• —————

The *Norland* normally operated as a ferry on the North Sea, and as such it was not anything like as luxurious as the *Canberra*, and had just enough accommodation for the two depleted Para Battalions. The ship did, however, provide me with my first shower in over a month. Brigadier Thompson, Commander of 3 Commando Brigade, came aboard to say goodbye before we sailed. He spoke of the close links formed between men of the red and green berets, but I doubted it, somehow. There will be rivalry between the two units as long as they both exist, and for the most part that is a positive thing that helps to maintain high standards.

We sailed steadily northwards, heading for Ascension Island, into better weather – and worse food. The cooks were not to blame – supplies were running low and rice became our staple diet. Luckily, I had rediscovered the art of reading books, and I was able to pass the time more easily in that way, as well as by joining in the trade of war souvenirs. I had a large collection of envelopes posted in Argentina, some with special stamps franked, 'Malvinas son Argentinas'. Dave 'Scoop' McGachen had not had the opportunity to acquire any souvenirs, so I gave him half of my envelope collection, which was promptly stolen from him.

The highlight of our journey to Ascension was the celebration to mark the annual 'Airborne Forces Day' – the first Saturday in July when Aldershot would host a reunion of the Airborne fraternity, the town's normally high quota of drunks would multiply several times, and the heroic tales of war experiences even more so. Our celebration on the *Norland* began with a sports competition. I took part in the orienteering event that was won, not surprisingly, by the ship's crew. Drinking began during the competition (in fact drinking was a part of it) and continued into the night. I celebrated with others in the bar designated as the Sergeants' Mess, and we had soon assembled a large pile of empty beer cans on our table. I stood on a table and sang a rugby song solo. That, and similar performances by others, obstructed a 2 Para Sergeant who tried in vain to organise a game of bingo. The floor of the Mess reverberated as the Toms on the deck below stood on tables and hammered on the ceiling with beer cans. The Toms were being entertained by one of the ship's crew who was performing some kind of drag act at the piano. As the evening cele-brations degenerated, the Toms did not allow the absence of Argentines or Royal Marines to get in the way of a good scrap – they fought each other. A brave member of the Sergeants' Mess decided that he would break up the fight on the deck below, but soon retreated with a bloody nose. When every beer can on board had been emptied, the party ended and the next day everyone agreed that, although not as good as a similar day in Aldershot, it had been a great success.

When we reached Ascension Island there was a wait until aircraft arrived to take us home. Gifts that had been sent to the Task Force from England were brought aboard. I searched through boxes of paperback books and found a bundle of military history books that had been donated by a man who had once fought with the Seaforth Highlanders. He had written his name and address in one of the books and beneath it, 'Please write'. I took some of the books but never bothered to write to him – later wishing that I had. There were also boxes of soap and shaving kit that had been sent by some women's organisation, and I helped myself to some of that.

On 5 July we were treated to a visit by General Sir Edwin Bram-mall, Chief of the General Staff, who had flown to Ascension to speak to us, and we all crammed into the dining hall to listen to his congratulations.

As transport aircraft arrived at Wideawake Airfield, men were ferried ashore by helicopters. The pilots found it easier to land on the

Norland when it was moving forwards rather than when it was at anchor, so we sailed back and forth across the anchorage. Dolphins swam alongside and dived over the waves at the bow, and I watched them for over an hour, feeling the warmth of the sun in my bones and aware for the first time since the war ended that I felt genuinely happy to have survived. I had helped to expel an invader from British territory. I had played the ultimate game and won.

As the first batches of Paras left the ship, they were replaced by men from a Scottish Regiment who were to be taken to the Falklands on the *Norland* to garrison the Islands. In the queue for meals one of the Scottish soldiers said loudly to his mates, 'They don't look like heroes to me!' It was the kind of remark that three months earlier would have been guaranteed to provoke a physical response from any Para, but now it was completely ignored.

My turn came to jump aboard a helicopter and leave the *Norland* for Wideawake Airfield, where I bought my allocation of spirits before boarding a VC10 in which I flew to RAF Brize Norton in Oxfordshire.

——— •◆• ———

As modern wars go, the Falklands Campaign had been a relatively clean fight. There was no use of toxic gas, napalm or fiendish booby-traps and other dirty tricks, and the civilian population did not suffer greatly (although three were accidentally killed in Stanley by 'friendly fire'). It had been clear to us who our enemy was and we had known where to find him, unlike our experiences in Ulster or, for example, the American experience in Vietnam. The Campaign was a short one; I had survived one night battle and two days of shelling, which in comparison to many other British campaigns in the past was really only a brief introduction to war. My curiosity was satisfied, and I came out of it a better soldier, knowing that if I went to war again I would do so with an equal determination but with none of the boyish enthusiasm with which I had approached this war. In some ways I was enriched by the experience; I felt privileged – in particular I felt an overwhelming pride in the fact that in the darkest hours of battle I had been sustained by the intrinsic belief that I was with men who were willing to give away life in unconditional sacrifice for each other.

207

I was, after much consideration and doubt, satisfied with my own performance – although I had identified certain things that I could have done better or differently. But, on the other side of the scales, I was also carrying home with me the indelible images of some of the scenes I had witnessed – unsought proof of the savage, uncivilised beast in us; a dark stain on my memory that might fade with time but one I would never be able to wash out entirely. It seems that it is impossible to enter a battlefield, even for a short time, and leave without being contaminated in some way.

When we landed in England, with the Falklands 8,000 miles behind us, I descended the steps from the aircraft to be greeted by a Colonel and a Warrant Officer from the Parachute Regiment. I recognised the Warrant Officer as one of the recruit staff who had trained me in the Depot 12 years earlier. As I walked across the apron to the terminal building I realised that I had forgotten to salute the Colonel. I carried with me the Argentine bag that had held my loot on Mount Longdon. The bag now contained washing and shaving kit, a paperback history of the Gallipoli Campaign from the old Seaforth Highlander, and a bottle of rum (duty-free).

KILLED IN ACTION ON MOUNT LONGDON

Private	RICHARD ABSOLON, MM
Private	GERALD BULL
Private	JASON BURT
Private	JONATHAN CROW
Private	MARK DODSWORTH
Private	ANTHONY GREENWOOD
Private	NEIL GROSE
Private	PETER HEDICKER
Lance Corporal	PETER HIGGS
Corporal	STEPHEN HOPE
Private	TIMOTHY JENKINS
Private	CRAIG JONES
Private	STEWART LAING
Lance Corporal	CHRISTOPHER LOVETT
Corporal	KEITH McCARTHY
Sergeant	IAN McKAY, VC
Lance Corporal	JAMES MURDOCH
Corporal	STEWART McLAUGHLIN
Lance Corporal	DAVID SCOTT
Private	IAN SCRIVENS
Craftsman	ALEXANDER SHAW
Private	PHILIP WEST
Corporal	SCOTT WILSON

———— •◆• ————

These hearts were woven of human joys and cares,
    Washed marvellously with sorrow, swift to mirth.
The years had given them kindness. Dawn was theirs,
    And sunset, and the colours of the earth.
These had seen movement, and heard music; known
    Slumber and waking; loved; gone proudly friended;
Felt the quick stir of wonder; sat alone;
    Touched flowers and furs and cheeks. All this is ended.
Rupert Brooke, 'The Dead'

Epilogue

It is not the critic who counts, not the man who points out how the strong man stumbles, or where the doer of deeds could have done them better. The credit belongs to the man who is actually in the arena, whose face is marred by dust and sweat and blood; who strives valiantly ... who knows the great enthusiasms, the great devotions; who spends himself in a worthy cause; who at the best knows in the end the triumph of high achievement, and who, at the worst, if he fails, at least fails while daring greatly – so that his place shall never be with those cold and timid souls who know neither victory nor defeat.

US President Theodore Roosevelt. Speech at the Sorbonne,
Paris, 1910

———— •◆• ————

The undeclared war for possession of the Falkland Islands lasted 74 days and claimed the lives of 256 men of the Task Force; 777 were wounded. The Argentines lost 746 killed and 1,053 wounded. Argentine losses on Mount Longdon are unclear, but it is believed that at least 30 died and 60 were wounded, with 50 being taken prisoner.

On our return to England we were all hailed as heroes – it had been, on the whole, a popular war. The nation was proud. We were not all heroes, of course – most of us had just done enough, and the majority of the true heroes were dead.

The dictator Leopoldo Galtieri was afterwards forced to resign, leading to the restoration of democracy in Argentina. In the United Kingdom, Margaret Thatcher rode the tide of national popularity to another election victory.

The General Purpose Machine-Gun was generally acknowledged by 3 Para as a whole to have been *the* battle-winning weapon. Shortly after our return to England the SF Machine-Gun Platoon was reformed in the Battalion, distinct from the Drums Platoon. Not long after that the British Army saw fit to withdraw the GPMG from service in infantry rifle sections. At the time of writing, it appears that the weapon may be re-introduced, if in smaller numbers.

The Metropolitan Police investigation into alleged atrocities on Mount Longdon was begun at the instigation of the Home Secretary in 1992. It was a lengthy, costly business (at a time when the police in Britain were seriously under-funded). The detectives made two visits to the Falkland Islands where they dug up the bodies of Argentines buried on Mount Longdon. The charade continued when the officers visited Argentina, and appeared on television there to plead with Argentine veterans of the Mount Longdon Battle to give evidence against British soldiers – the Argentines refused to cooperate. The police report was passed to the Director of Public Prosecutions, who wisely decided that it was not in the public interest to pursue a prosecution.

I believe that about fifty prisoners were taken by 3 Para on Mount Longdon – many of them could have been justifiably killed during our night attack. If they are alive today it is because the men of 3 Para decided that they ought to be.

The SS *Canberra* was sold by P & O and left Southampton for the last time on 11 October 1997 and sailed to Karachi, Pakistan, where she was broken up for scrap. The job was expected to take three months, but despite five hundred men working day and night with steel cutting machinery, the ship resisted for well over a year.

At the time of writing, for the twentieth anniversary of the conflict, Argentina still lays claim to the Falkland Islands, which are garrisoned by a British force of around two thousand troops – almost equivalent to the size of the local population.

Tony and Ailsa Heathman still live at Estancia House. The 'Rumour Control HQ' sign I made for the trench I occupied at Estancia now hangs in the porch of the farmhouse there.

'Dave', who drove the tractor that transported our Milan equipment from Teal Inlet to Estancia, is Dave Thorsen, who still lives and works at Teal Settlement.

Sergeant Chris Howard, Anti-tank Platoon, 3 Para served in all three regular Battalions of the Parachute Regiment after 1982, as well as the 4th Volunteer Battalion. He retired from the Army after 22 years' service in 1994 with the rank of Warrant Officer Class 2, and then undertook a course in deer management, which he passed with distinction and won the college trophy for best student. Chris is married with a son aged 17 and a daughter aged 20. He works as a deer-stalker at Petworth Park in Sussex with Badger and Rolo, two faithful four-legged hunting companions.

Colour Sergeant Steve 'Shakespeare' Knights, Anti-tank Platoon, 3 Para served for a total of 27 years in the Parachute Regiment. He was commissioned in 1993, served three tours on active service in Bosnia and retired with the rank of Captain in 1997. He then spent two years as a contract manager for a security firm ('it was crap') before rejoining the Army as a Full Time Reserve Service officer. He is now a Captain at the Royal Military Academy, Sandhurst.

Corporal Martin 'Taff (the Jap)' Richardson, Anti-tank Platoon, 3 Para continued to serve in the Battalion's 'Anti-tanks' and eventually commanded the Milan Platoon. He also served in the 4th Volunteer Battalion in addition to serving for two years in a parachute trials unit. He retired from the Army in 1996 after 23 years' service with the rank of Colour Sergeant. During his time as a civilian his various forms of employment have included: removing eco-warriors from various sites of protest around the country; dismantling scaffolding at the Atlanta Olympic Games; helping to build the A465 as a JCB operator; driving children to school in a double-decker bus; working as a supermarket security guard and labouring on a building site. He now sells microlite aircraft. He lives in South Wales.

The Argentine recoilless anti-tank gun 'captured' by Taff Richardson and me was brought back to England and it is now proudly displayed by 3 Para in their barracks. It is the commonly held but mistaken belief that it was captured on Mount Longdon.

Corporal Mick Mathews, Anti-tank Platoon, was killed in a terrorist bomb explosion while on active service in Ulster on 27 July 1988.

Private Andy 'Stretch' Dunn left 3 Para in 1987 with the rank of Lance-Corporal, and joined the Police Service. He is now the Senior Firearms Instructor of a Tactical Firearms Unit with the North Wales Police. He is married with a 10-year-old daughter and in his spare time he is a mountain rescue search dog-handler; so when not dealing with firearms incidents he is often called to search for missing climbers on Mount Snowdon.

The Parachute Regiment still has three regular Battalions, although two of its Territorial Army Battalions have been disbanded. Since the Falklands Campaign the Regiment has served with distinction in the Balkans and Sierra Leone, and forms the backbone of 16 Air Assault Brigade, based at Colchester. The Pegasus emblem, symbol of British airborne forces since the Second World War, has been abandoned in favour of an eagle, more typical of German airborne units.

I retired from the Regular Army in 1992 after 23 years' service. I immediately joined the Territorial Army, and at 48 years of age I continue to throw myself from aeroplanes and generally train for the next war. I am married with a son and two daughters. I serve in a British Army that, since I joined it over thirty years ago, has continued to be weakened by successive manpower cuts. If there is one obvious lesson that history ought to have taught us, it is that wars will have to be fought on a regular basis, and the best thing to do is to maintain armed forces that are strong enough (with the right political backing) to deter would-be aggressors, and strong enough to bring those wars that have to be fought to a swift conclusion. The world has not become a safer place since the end of the Cold War, and short-term savings that have been made by weakening our forces will cost us dearly in the long run – both financially and, more importantly, in terms of human suffering.

Time to get down from my soapbox and, old soldier that I am, fade away. I think it appropriate that the last words should come from others.

Last Words

Vernon Steen acted as a guide to SP Company during the recce patrol to Mount Longdon on 5 June 1982.

'My family and I had returned to the Falklands in March 1980 following a three-year stint in Perth, Scotland where I had been training as an Aircraft Engineer. We settled very easily back into the familiar life and surroundings we had grown up in. Our three children, aged between eleven and seven years, were equally pleased. The Falklands have a unique and stark beauty that I have never experienced anywhere else. It's a place where you can go where your nose takes you and the scenery stretches your eyeballs.

'After three years' training I was eager to get back to work with the Falkland Islands Government Air Service (FIGAS). Engineering was my one love, and now that I had qualified I needed some practical work to get rid of the stress and frustration of the long period of training.

'The political situation was one that I kept an eye on, and having been a member of the Falkland Islands Committee I liked to think that my political awareness was reasonably sharp. During the year following our return various eminent British politicians tried to persuade the Falkland Islanders that their best interests lay in ceding sovereignty to Argentina. We were told by Nicholas Ridley of the Foreign Office at a public meeting in November 1980 that if we persisted in our stance then "blood would be spilt in the Islands". The political situation took a nose-dive over the next several months, but not in my wildest dreams did I ever consider that Argentina would opt for the violent course of action it embarked on, on 2 April 1982. Thereafter survival became the order of the day; everybody did what they felt was appropriate to ensure the well-being of family and friends.

'Liberation Day was a godsend; talk about relief. However, so much chaos and confusion reigned during those early days after the fighting had stopped, that one lived on permanent adrenaline. The invading forces had destroyed all three aircraft belonging to FIGAS and our hangar was like a colander. However, regardless of its condition, the Army Air Corps was thankful for the facility. It was better than working out in the weather at that time of the year.

'Until we got our first aircraft in late December 1982, I threw in my lot with whoever wanted to use me. The ground staff of FIGAS acquired a captured Argentinian helicopter (ex-US Army UH1H Huey) which we secured with no objection from the British Military Authority. Welcome help came from the Aircraft Engineering Officer, Lieutenant Commander Caesley from HMS *Invincible*, who very kindly offered us assistance to get the helicopter serviceable. This came in the form of Chief Petty Officer Al Downham, Petty Officer George Pilch and friends. After several days Lieutenant Commander Keith Dudley was able to fly the helicopter, first to San Carlos and then on to *Invincible* for some tender loving care. Some weeks later, in full FIGAS colours and with Falklands registration VP-FBD, she was delivered back to Stanley.

'Major Bob Connel (a Canadian exchange pilot serving with the Army Air Corps) undertook to fly mail and freight around the camp, supplementing some of the previous activities that FIGAS had carried out. Then bureaucracy overtook us: with normalisation setting in, the Ministry of Defence was reluctant to permit its aircrew to fly a 'civil' aircraft. Sadly the helicopter was grounded after only two flights. However, it kept us occupied and helped make new friends with all those who assisted with the venture.

'In late December 1982 our first aircraft, a de Havilland Beaver, arrived in a 40-foot container. This we had flying by 20 January 1983, re-commencing service, primarily mail and freight, during the next week. Delivery was taken during March 1983 of two Britten-Norman Islanders. The first passenger flight was carried out on 1 April 1983, one year after the invasion. Normal service was once again resumed.

'I was still finding it difficult, 18 months after the conflict, to come to terms with the happenings of those long 74 days of occupation. I had met many people during the campaign to re-take Stanley, and made some great friends, too numerous to mention; some, so sadly, to die in that action. Seeing life from a new and overwhelming perspective of war, with all its horrors, brings the realisation of how easily one can fall into the trap of taking life for granted. Each moment should be cherished as if it's your last, because it just might be.

'The process of putting one's life back together again cannot be put on hold forever, reality soon kicks in, things to do, bills to pay, places to go. The transition back to normality took time but thankfully we, as a family, supported one another. Work obviously helped. Our fourth child, Kimberley, was born on 9 June 1985. Also in 1985, I became Chief Engineer of FIGAS and General Manager in 1990.

'Time has helped heal the scars but the memories will be with us to the grave. A momentous event occurred on 14 July 2000, when Falkland Councillors stood alongside their British and Argentinian counterparts and signed an Agreement permitting, among other things, access to the Falklands by Argentinian nationals. I hope this has shown the world the resolve of the Falkland people, that despite the events of 1982, we are willing to reach out a hand of friendship. The posturing of the recently elected Argentinian Government has however done little to bolster our confidence, but I hope the ordinary Argentinian folk realise that a harmonious relationship is to the benefit of both nationalities.

'On 14 June 2002 the Falkland Islanders will commemorate the 20th anniversary of the liberation of our Islands. While plans are at an early stage, I hope as many people who were involved with the successful outcome of the conflict will make the pilgrimage back to pay tribute, with us, to those whose lives were lost. I hope they will savour the moment in time and decide for themselves its worth. I look forward to renewing so many friendships.'

Lance-Corporal Denzil 'the Hump' Connick served with Anti-tank Platoon, 3 Para, during the Falklands conflict.

'I was hit by shell fire on the evening of 13 June 1982, just one day prior to the ceasefire. However, none of us knew at the time that the war would soon be over. As far as any of us were concerned, we still had a long hard fight ahead of us, street fighting through the town of Stanley.

'The shell that got me – and killed the two young lads who just happened to be chatting with me – blew off my left leg just above the knee, and my other leg was in tatters. I remained conscious throughout the whole terrible episode. I was soon taken in an army

216

Scout helicopter to Fitzroy field hospital. I was very lucky to have the luxury of a helicopter casevac – choppers were a rare commodity and I would have been dead without it.

'I sailed around the Islands for about four weeks on the hospital ship *Uganda*. I underwent a number of operations and painful treatment of my wounds. It was quite an experience on the ship. Lying in a hospital bed in a room that moved was weird. Argie casualties were in beds amongst us British ones. We took their beer rations off them; other than that, they were treated exactly the same as us, with plenty of TLC.

'On return to dear old England I was kept alive and well fed at the Queen Elizabeth's Military Hospital in Woolwich, London. I spent some six months there, on and off, before being sent home to Chepstow on indefinite sick leave, pending discharge from the army. I "ceased to fulfil the medical standards required" in May 1984 and was then a civvy.

'Thanks to the grateful British public, a fund was created to help the families of those killed and those of us who were wounded, called the South Atlantic Fund. I received, through the post, a cheque that resembled a pools win. It was very exciting to be rich, newly married with a baby son (proof that one small appendage was still working) and poised to tackle the world of commerce.

'I began a franchise with the "Cookie Coach Company", a van sales operation wholesaling home style snacks and confections to the independent trade. I did this dressed in a red jacket and straw boater hat, with a van that was customised to look like a 1920s delivery van. I looked a complete prat! However, I really hoped I would be successful. The business failed a year later along with a car repair venture that I had started in parallel with the Cookie Coach business. The losses were caused by the activities of business associates and the simple economics of trying to run a business in South Wales during the miners' strike of 1984–5.

'I then became a financial adviser/insurance salesman. I had learned the hard way in business and was very keen to make sure people never made the same mistakes as I had, particularly my old friends from the Regiment. I did this until the 1990s with various levels of success, but the work was hard and often without much reward. I became very ill with an infection that had lain dormant since

217

my injuries in 1982. This was, in a way, a blessing in disguise. It forced me to give up my work permanently, relieving me of all the hassle and trouble of being self-employed. I was given an increase to my war pension, enough to get along with, and, with the assistance of SSAFA, the Airborne Forces Security Fund and Colonel Simon Brewis (now a great friend), was helped to settle properly in a new home (a bungalow).

'Simon Brewis was the CO of the Depot, Parachute Regiment in 1982. He was also an officer with 3 Para before that. Simon suggested that I become a volunteer caseworker for SSAFA to help occupy my mind, which was becoming stale with boredom. I enjoyed this work immensely and it taught me an awful lot about the cruel treatment of our ex-service people, who are often left to their fates, unnoticed.

'In April 1997 the South Atlantic Medal Association (82) was formed on my initiative with Dr Rick Jolly, Lieutenant-Colonel Tony Davis, Lieutenant-General Sir Hew Pike, Mrs Sara Jones, Lieutenant-Colonel Simon Brewis and Major-General Julian Thompson. SAMA 82 is now a flourishing veterans' association with many hundreds represented from throughout the 1982 Task Force. I am now the Secretary of SAMA and enjoy the busy everyday business of looking after the varied interests of the Association and its membership.'

Ailsa Heathman still lives at Estancia House.

'Tony and I have remained at Estancia, having bought the farm in 1980. We have been married for 23 years and have two daughters. Nyree was born in 1981 and had her first birthday in the middle of the war. Fortunately she had started walking just before so wasn't crawling around in all the muck that ended up in the house. Tara was in the planning stage when the Argentines invaded so was hastily postponed until we saw the outcome – she was born in 1983.

'Both our girls survived on the excellent camp education system whereby they had daily radio lessons for half an hour or more. Their radio teachers set them more work daily and their rotten mother would not let them out until each day's homework was done – so they soon learned not to play up too much! That served them from age four to ten/eleven when they moved to Stanley. Because we were so close to Stanley, they were lucky enough to be able to come home each weekend. They boarded through the week in Stanley House Hostel for camp kids – so they had the best of both worlds.

'The schools and hospital are very well resourced thanks to the income from the fishing industry, created in 1986 as a result of the war and the establishment of a 200-mile exclusion zone. It has enhanced life in many ways for people on the Islands. A few will still moan that fishing has done nothing for them personally but life has improved beyond measure and people's expectations have risen considerably – in some ways that is sad and I worry that our kids have never known anything but the good life they now enjoy. The price of progress – I guess.

'The new hospital and the new Community School were built to the tune of £12 million each and I honestly believe we enjoy services second to none for a community this size. Any medical cases that cannot be treated here are sent to the UK, and real emergencies are medevaced to Montevideo in Uruguay by Hercules, courtesy of the RAF.

'We also now enjoy a road network around most of East Falkland and a large part of West Falkland, both still under construction. It is possible to circumnavigate the whole of East Falkland in a day now, quite comfortably. It would have made life much easier in 1982, but then the Argentines would not have been confined to a few areas either.

'Tony and I are still struggling with the farm but the bottom fell out of the wool market 10–12 years ago and small farms are no longer viable. Many would have gone to the wall but the new-found healthy economy meant that the Falkland Islands Government could support us with subsidies and various grant schemes. We were all encouraged to diversify but that is easier said than done, given that the local market for any product is very small and we are not really able to produce enough of anything to make export viable. A new EEC-standard abattoir is presently being built and the powers that be have big plans for it so we will see what happens.

'We have branched into a bit of tourism, doing tours for a couple of local operators, and have been looking to expand on that. We also expanded our gardens and that did very well last year but we had a poor year this year. We are also growing tomatoes but they are not the answer we were led to believe although there is no problem getting rid of them. Hay has been another form of diversification and we had a good crop this year but had such a struggle to get it baled in the bad weather, which has also hampered the tomato ripening.

'Tony has been quite involved with pasture improvement for a few years now so we have used that for some fat lambs and the hay, and we also sell some mutton throughout the winter, and we have a friend whom we supply with sausage meat so we can just about survive! Tony also earns a little extra money by shearing sheep of the National Stud Flock, and acts as a guide to an Australian chap who is here looking for gold, diamonds and other minerals, on the grounds that we were once attached to Africa. They have found some gold so we are all waiting and hoping; likewise with the prospective oil industry. Now the price of oil has risen again, we may see some renewed activity. When the rig was here a few years ago the price of oil fell so drastically that it wasn't viable to keep it any longer, but the data they collected are reported to look promising.

'Nyree now works as an observer with the local air service (FIGAS). She flies in the Islander and logs all ships, licences, positions, etc. Last year she spotted a few poachers, one of whom was arrested and brought here so she had to give evidence in court. Tara works as an accounts clerk in the Falkland Islands Company Office. Both Nyree and Tara earn as much as we get from the wool!

'So, all in all, the Argentines did us a favour in 1982, but that does not mean that we can forget the sacrifices that were made for us. We all owe each and every member of the Task Force more than we can ever hope to repay.'

SAMA 82 exists to help veterans of the South Atlantic campaign and to strengthen links with the people of the Falkland Islands. The SAMA 82 website can be found at: http://www.sama82.org.uk and contains a timeline of campaign events and a 'Garden of Remembrance' which gives details of the men of the Task Force and Falkland Islanders who were killed.

A proportion of the author's royalties from this book will be donated to SAMA 82.

Index